How Libraries Make Tough Choices
in Difficult Times

CHANDOS

INFORMATION PROFESSIONAL SERIES

Series Editor: Ruth Rikowski
(Email: Rikowskigr@aol.com)

Chandos' new series of books is aimed at the busy information professional. They have been specially commissioned to provide the reader with an authoritative view of current thinking. They are designed to provide easy-to-read and (most importantly) practical coverage of topics that are of interest to librarians and other information professionals. If you would like a full listing of current and forthcoming titles, please visit our website, www.chandospublishing.com, email wp@woodheadpublishing.com or telephone +44 (0) 1223 499140.

New authors: we are always pleased to receive ideas for new titles; if you would like to write a book for Chandos, please contact Dr Glyn Jones on gjones@chandospublishing.com or telephone +44 (0) 1993 848726.

Bulk orders: some organisations buy a number of copies of our books. If you are interested in doing this, we would be pleased to discuss a discount. Please email wp@woodheadpublishing.com or telephone +44 (0) 1223 499140.

How Libraries Make Tough Choices in Difficult Times

Purposeful abandonment

DAVID STERN

CP

CHANDOS
PUBLISHING

Oxford Cambridge New Delhi

Chandos Publishing
Hexagon House
Avenue 4
Station Lane
Witney
Oxford OX28 4BN
UK
Tel: +44(0) 1993 848726
Email: info@chandospublishing.com
www.chandospublishing.com
www.chandospublishingonline.com

Chandos Publishing is an imprint of Woodhead Publishing Limited

Woodhead Publishing Limited
80 High Street
Sawston
Cambridge CB22 3HJ
UK
Tel: +44(0) 1223 499140
Fax: +44(0) 1223 832819
www.woodheadpublishing.com

First published in 2013

ISBN: 978-1-84334-701-9 (print)

ISBN: 978-1-78063-367-1 (online)

British Library Cataloguing-in-Publication Data.
A catalogue record for this book is available from the British Library.

Typeset by RefineCatch Ltd, Bungay, Suffolk
Printed in the UK and USA.

Printed in the UK by 4edge Ltd, Hockley, Essex.

Contents

List of figures

List of case studies

Acknowledgements

There are many people who deserve recognition for the content within this short monograph.

First, I wish to thank all those who have attempted to mentor me. To those who have willingly and generously given their time and their perspective I will always remain grateful. To those who have provided unsolicited advice, I will forever remember those concepts and the feelings they generated in me. Those who have served as mentors through intentionally or unwittingly demonstrating the good and the bad, the powers and dangers, and the obvious and the subtle aspects of management, I thank you for the lessons. It is better to learn from the management mistakes of others whenever possible, rather than to experience them yourself. But some lessons must be learned through first-hand experience.

Secondly, I wish to thank all those colleagues who have suffered through my learning experiences. I offer my deepest respects to those who have trusted me (or perhaps not) and who have provided important feedback in many ways and with great patience. Just as I was once helpful to others in their development, I owe a great deal to those who I have experimented upon. I hope my lessons were not too painful for you. I thank my colleagues all along the way for the support that has made this book possible. I also recognize all those who have made this book necessary.

Special thanks must be given to my fellow Special Libraries Association colleagues who provided a risk-free environment in which to discover and explore both the traditional and newest forms of communication, collaboration, programming, and decision-making. Your enthusiasm, patience, and knowledge are only surpassed by your kindness and your professionalism.

Finally, I cannot imagine completing this effort without the support of my better half, my dear wife Susan, who has nursed me through the failures and stood beside me (and is more than partly responsible) for many of my successes. I could never hope to find a better partner, collaborator, and conspirator.

About the author

David Stern is Associate Dean for Public Services at Illinois State University.

Responsible for administering a $7 million resources budget with oversight for the work of 23 librarians and support staff, as a member of the Library's senior administrative team he plays a lead role in library-wide planning and evaluation and in setting the Library's strategic directions.

David Stern was the founder and principal of *Maximize Information*, a firm specializing in advanced information discovery techniques, enhancing organizational communication, collaboration and knowledge management, and leading organizational reviews and project management initiatives to find service quality improvements. He was the Associate University Librarian for Scholarly Resources at Brown University, the Director of Science Libraries at Yale University and he has also worked as a general librarian, a medical librarian, and a science librarian in centralized and departmental libraries. In addition, he has taught library science graduate courses (University of Illinois and Southern Connecticut State University) and serves as a consultant and advisor to a number of professional societies and commercial publishers and online services. He has degrees in Biological Sciences (University of Connecticut), History & Philosophy of Science (Indiana University), and Library Science (Indiana University).

David served on the Board of Directors (2000–2003) and as the Chair of the Knowledge Management Division (2007–2008) of the Special Libraries Association, the leading international library association of over 9,000 librarians serving specialized populations of researchers. He is currently the Chair of the Virtual Worlds Advisory Council.

David also served as Editor of the journal *Science and Technology Libraries* from 2005–2007. His research involves electronic retrieval and transmission of data, focused primarily upon scholars' workstations. He was recently involved in the development of end-user search systems for both local and remote hosts, including a web-based expert systems librarian emulator and linking of paleobotany fulltext material with related museum and researcher databases. He is also working on the development of standards and cost models for federated full-text search and retrieval systems.

His publications include over a dozen journal articles, several book chapters, two edited special issues of *Science and Technology Libraries*, and the book *Guide to Information Sources in the Physical Sciences* (Colorado: Libraries Unlimited, 2000).

He has been a speaker at conferences of ALA, SLA, AAAS, SSP, ASIS, NASIG, Online, InfoToday, Computers in Libraries, Charleston Conference, CESSE, NFAIS, and the Library of Congress.

The author may be contacted at:
email: *hdavid.stern@gmail.com*

Introduction

The intention of this book is to serve two distinct populations of library staff. The first group of readers are those unfamiliar with basic management techniques in libraries, be they staff members or new administrators. For this group the book provides some considerations and techniques that have been developed through years of management training and sometimes painful experience. My hope is to offer guidance to both those being supervised and beginning supervisors. This information may also be helpful for newly appointed middle managers moving into more administrative positions.

The second group of targeted readers are experienced managers. My hope is to help busy managers perhaps discover some new tools and remember considerations that they may not always keep in mind as they work through their daily business. Perhaps browsing this book will remind them to see the larger aspects and incorporate particular elements of continual service reviews that are important to employ in order to develop and maintain a high performing organization.

This type of overview is offered as a practical guide for managers operating under difficult financial pressures. It concentrates on selected methods to identify priorities and to revise operations. The goal is to demonstrate sensitivity to user needs and to demonstrate the value of creativity and participatory decision making in allocating limited resources. No attempt is made to mention all, or even a full range, of the management tools and techniques that exist. To obtain a more complete coverage of the much larger suite of management techniques I would suggest reading management texts designed for librarians. I have included just a few relevant example materials within the book as "Suggested readings". By no means do these few suggestions provide an adequate overview of the best materials to be reviewed. For serious reading on the topics mentioned in this book there are many journal articles, business case studies, and books about general management techniques. There are also entire sets of published materials about specific tools and techniques for the various aspects of communication, planning, project management, assessment, and personnel concerns that are discussed in this book. Plan to make professional development a career project, and continue to seek out new tools and techniques through the literature, professional development training, and through mentoring relationships.

We all dream of having a seat at the Round Table in Camelot, or at least of listening to the conversations like a fly on the wall. Everyone wants to be in the know, if not directly involved, in important decisions that have an impact on their life. Most people do not want to sit in meetings that provide meaningless outcomes in relation to their own personal interests. Concerns arise when people are not certain of what is being discussed and how these decisions might impact them directly. There will be fewer requests to sit at the big table if your organization has transparent meetings and adequate employee involvement in day-to-day decisions. If systems are developed that generate trust and respect there will be far fewer conflicts and barriers to progress. The goal of good management is to increase participation in decision making whenever and wherever it is advantageous so there are few surprises and excellent group dynamics. The camaraderie that develops will allow you to work together in difficult times to accomplish more than the bare minimum by consistently concentrating your efforts and resources on clearly defined and understood user-oriented priorities. This book contains suggestions that might help to create such pleasant and productive work environments. It also reminds managers to focus on outreach to users and stakeholders to obtain essential feedback as well as support and advocacy.

Case examples are included throughout the text to serve as demonstrations of these tools and techniques in practical situations. These examples describe how shared analysis and deeply considered service modifications have occurred and have resulted in improved services and demonstrated effective management and leadership.

I hope this book serves you well as a learning and stimulation tool, and as a reference tool, as you embark upon a successful and satisfying career as a fully engaged participant within a high performing organization.

Considered and effective leadership

Abstract: Difficult fiscal scenarios can be seen as opportunities to make difficult but necessary choices. External pressures can create a climate that will spur your organization to become more flexible and agile. Use unintended and undesirable circumstances to move your organization further along the path toward becoming a high performing organization, developing a culture that is even more responsive to user needs and expectations. Undertaking a complete organizational review can be time intensive and unsettling, but if done correctly, it can also be cleansing, invigorating, and helpful for staff morale. The result of incorporating purposeful abandonment will be a more effective organization, with an appreciative clientele and a realistic set of priorities and operations.

Key words: high performing organization, purposeful abandonment, external pressures, service reviews, financial difficulties, opportunities, enhancements.

Why undertake a review?

As the economist Paul Romer stated, "Don't let a good crisis go to waste."

Consider your current difficult fiscal scenario as an opportunity to make difficult but necessary choices with less emotional resistance. Utilize the pressured climate to spur your organization to become even more flexible and agile. Use this unintended and undesirable impetus to develop a culture even more responsive to user needs and expectations. In reality, these are all desirable traits of a high-performing organization.

Undertaking a complete organizational review can be time intensive and frightening, but if done correctly, it can also be cleansing, invigorating, and helpful for staff morale. A well-conceived organizational review begins with considering and determining the ultimate intentions. Will the organization be satisfied if it continues to for the most part operate and perform as before, simply saving money after an efficiency re-engineering process? Or is this the right time to perform a more transformational evaluation and redesign, possibly abandoning less important operations while supplementing and/or enhancing existing services? A thorough organizational review should at least consider implementing transformational changes rather than merely modifying existing operations; even more so when resources are limited and new services are still expected. Purposeful abandonment of selected operations will be the logical consequence of intentionally using tough times as a driving force to examine, re-evaluate and drop certain historical but not recently re-evaluated tasks.

Organizational reviews may be initiated due to both internal and external factors. Changes in local conditions and priorities may result in reduced resource levels, or uncontrollable external costs may drive efforts to review and revise existing operations. Often it is both local competition and outside influences that pressure the organization, and the best ways to combat these factors are to be aware of potential stresses and proactively offer solutions that demonstrate your awareness of other competing claims on resources and concurrently enhance your services in important areas. Justifying budgets to simply maintain the status quo will not be as successful as offering better services with the same budget requests. Be seen as creative and entrepreneurial rather than conservative and safe.

Managing expectations, not operations

A library is a service organization, and success should be measured by the quality of the services provided. Quality can be measured in many ways – efficiency, effectiveness, satisfaction, creativity, and flexibility and agility to adapt in changing times. The most important element of success is the generation of user support and advocacy. In the highly competitive resource allocation negotiations that occur during challenging financial times, administrations often consider testimonials very highly ... perhaps even more importantly than raw numbers which carry no inherent values. Powerful justifications and requests for additional or continuing resources should include important and informed stakeholder support.

In terms of documenting excellence, it is more important to measure and demonstrate user services effectiveness and satisfaction rather than internal productivity and efficiencies. For this reason you will want to solicit user feedback in quantitative and qualitative ways. It is also important to perform organized Focus Group and ethnological studies to better understand user desires and behaviors. This will help you create a more user-oriented organization.

Demonstrating user satisfaction with services is not enough; administrators also expect high-performing organizations to maximize their capital resources by considering and intelligently repurposing public spaces in relation to user desires and changing behaviors. Creatively adapting physical spaces and equipment is an important part of demonstrating good management, and leads to trust and respect – which leads to better and more proactive relationships with decision makers.

In addition to satisfying user expectations and making obvious facilities enhancements, addressing and meeting internal staff expectations results in improved morale. In addition, the involvement of staff in the design and evaluation of operations, with their detailed and nuanced understandings of day-to-day specific operations, often results in more highly improved and enhanced services. One cannot overestimate the importance and influence of total staff involvement in organizational reviews.

Finally, while libraries would like to control the environment and domain of expectations, in these dynamic times user expectations are often developed in response to outside factors, known as disruptive influences, which are outside the control of the library or the organization. These external influences must be identified and considered if libraries are to remain relevant portals and spaces for ever-changing user needs and desires.

Reporting to multiple masters: finding a balance of service quality and efficiencies

Libraries exist with a perpetual state of conflicting interests. In the classic paradigm, libraries must spend money to save researchers and users time and effort . . . which are often not counted as values in a measurable and returnable way. Good managers make such returns on investments obvious and part of the value equation.

Academic libraries are in a difficult and delicate situation as either cost centers or non-fee operations. Frequently a challenging administrative question is, "To whom do you demonstrate success?"

On the one hand, the administration stresses efficiency through efforts at centralization and standardization. On the other hand, user populations request customization and specialized services. The result is often a balancing of costs and services, with specialized services maintained according to specific population needs and demands. The consolidation of service points, a reduction in branch or departmental libraries, and the centralization of cataloging, check-in, and other distributed services are becoming more prevalent due to financial concerns. Fewer departments maintain librarian subject specialists as libraries migrate toward standardized book and journal profiles, patron-driven acquisitions, and/ or utilize consortial cooperation for collection development and reference assistance. The expansion of e-books, with the possibility for on-demand point-of-need document delivery, will also allow for the further removal of redundancy of staff and services to unique and distributed populations. Librarians must advocate for and demonstrate a strong need for specialized and distributed services in order to maintain these more expensive (but more satisfying) arrangements.

Quite often politics and history are just as important as actual service quality when departments consider closing a branch library or removing subject support staff. As a decision maker, do not always allow emotional considerations to override practical or political concerns that may have much more important long-term value and impact. Lead users into the future with sensitive but firm direction and information about the need and benefits of change. Lead users across the uncomfortable line with the knowledge that new options will improve their efforts and resulting services.

Use quick demonstrations to show such improvements; seeing actual and powerful new options rather than hearing about them will quickly make converts out of even the most stubborn holdouts.

Commercial libraries may not have the exact same confusion of priorities, but they are constantly being reviewed for effectiveness in comparison to free resources and outsourced information services. Charge-back mechanisms to individual corporate units and enterprise-wide services for international operations can be just as competitive and require careful balances of special interests. In these cases the return on the investment (ROI) is even more important to demonstrate, and is the best way to compete against free options that might actually carry heavy negative costs in terms of effectiveness, reliability, and credibility.

Involvement and understandings across the organization

In order to perform a successful evaluation of the current operation the entire staff should be involved in the review process. A successful review process starts by involving the staff in these discussions from the very start. The key to active staff buy-in is transparent communication throughout the entire process. Important stages for all-staff inclusion are: considering the ultimate goals of the review, defining the terminology to be used, identifying the available resources and hindrances to progress, allocating expertise and enthusiasm, discovering best practices, determining and measuring the success of the outcomes, proactively retraining staff when their jobs are modified and/or eliminated, and recording and sharing lessons learned. The process should appear well conceived, designed, and managed, and should provide for continuous feedback and review once any modifications are made.

Each individual review process should be seen as part of a larger organizational plan and all staff should understand the logic of the underlying strategic approach. Each staff member should see both the ultimate organizational goals and how their efforts function as aligned tasks within their own unit's priorities. Existing operations should be seen in terms of best practices and staff should develop a desire for adopting new tools, trends and services that improve efficiencies, offer better user services, and make their work more productive and interesting.

When an entire staff are motivated and acting in unison you will see far greater creativity and awareness, which will result in deeper penetration and improved morale and productivity. Even casual observers and visitors will notice a positive work environment.

The four Ds: Do, Delegate, Delay, Drop

Regardless of the decision-making process that is utilized, once prioritization has been determined, it is time to assign resources, administrative responsibilities, and advocacy tasks. All existing operations, plus potential new services, should be assigned to one of the following categories:

- Do – perform this operation at the highest level of capability with constant top-level feedback and support.
- Delegate – assign the operation to a sub-unit and expect updates and requests for additional resources if measurable outcomes are not reached.
- Delay – postpone the implementation until a later (and designated) review time.

- Drop – stop performing this task as it is no longer an organizational priority. At this stage of Purposeful Abandonment the associated resources can be reapplied to other priority tasks with greater impact.

Project management

Project management is where most organizations fail to achieve their intended objectives. They may identify appropriate goals, but they do not create the necessary structure to reach that new level of service due to unintended and paralyzing barriers or due to a failure of authorities to adequately address competing interests. The correct implementation of a project management process leads to some level of success regardless of barriers, and over time creates a more powerful learning organization.

Once the project plan has been developed, and the assignment of project responsibilities has been designated, it is time to create either hierarchical reporting lines or one-time project management support plans. Some on-going services or operations are logical candidates for either short-term project management reviews or more extensive service quality reviews. The programmatic identification of resources, best practices, evaluation benchmarks, and feedback processes will facilitate an orderly and successful service rollout or review.

Decision-making skills and implications

Even the best plans can become failures if there are not a well-developed set of critical decision-making skills directing operations. A clear plan, consistency in administrative support, appropriate group involvement and real-time learning, cross-unit collaboration and communication, and regular staff and user feedback is required to bring the best plans to fruition, and to ensure that initial operations continue to satisfy changing user needs over time. This may require across the board staff training in many aspects of teamwork, brainstorming, communication, management, and administration. This shared decision making requires a delicate balancing of administrative oversight and direction and staff operational leadership. Different situations require different problem-solving tools, and an organization should have a toolkit of processes that are employed when appropriate. It is important to have the correct data and techniques to address particular situations. Many organizations invest in regular training programs in order to develop a cadre of in-house staff with a broad array of decision-making skills; other organizations outsource facilitation teams and hire consulting firms when high-level analysis and decision-making skills are required.

2

Preparing for analysis

Abstract: It is surprising how often organizations attack a symptom rather than the cause of a problem. The best way to approach a problem situation is to harness the full power of an organization to analyze the conditions. Key questions must be asked about ultimate intentions . . . Is the organization only interested in making modifications in order to save money? Does the organization want to make this situation into an opportunity to improve and/or enhance services? Is the organization willing to shake up the culture and modify historical activities in order to make transformational change rather than simply transitional improvements? These questions must be answered before any actions are taken in order to understand which modifications should be considered. Do not waste time exploring options that you are not prepared to implement for political or other reasons, and do not raise expectations and set unreachable goals when resources will not be available or adequate for the desired outcomes. Quality analysis is an ongoing process that begins with recognition, communication, and shared data gathering.

Key words: analysis, service reviews, intentions, re-engineering, vision, expectations.

Failure is easy, success takes thoughtful effort

In many organizations comprehensive reviews are doomed from their earliest stages. Quite often projects fail because the project was mis-directed from the start. The underlying issue was not adequately identified, described, evaluated, or modified. It is surprising how often organizations attack a symptom rather than the cause of the problem. It is no wonder that the results of such projects fail to adequately provide long-term corrections.

The best way to approach a solution is to bring to the situation a clear goal, the full power of the organization, the strong support of the administration, and the conviction to make serious modifications if they are needed.

Understanding the Mission and objectives of your organization

The first step in any successful organizational review and revision process is to understand the actual goals; in other words, to determine the intentions of your future actions. Is the organization only interested in making modifications in order to save money? Does the organization want to make this situation into an opportunity to improve and/or enhance services? Is the organization willing to shake up the culture and modify historical activities in order to make transformational change rather than simply transitional improvements? Perhaps multiple intentions are involved for different areas of the complete review. These questions must be asked and answered honestly before any actions are begun in order to understand how seriously to explore all possible modifications and how deeply to reconsider all existing operations. Do not waste time exploring options that you are not prepared to implement for political or other reasons, and do not raise expectations and set unreachable goals when resources will not be available or adequate for the desired outcomes.

In the case below you will observe how an organization must develop an understanding of intentions and expand expectations in order to become a more flexible and agile organization. Inspiration must be nurtured, encouraged, and rewarded.

Case Study 1: Vision versus Mission

A new Library Director arrives and gathers her people together to understand the hopes and dreams of the staff. She searches across the library and discovers stated service intentions and public statements of service quality expectations. After reviewing the posted Mission statement and the Strategic Planning documents, she realizes that there has never been a Vision document. She asks for the creation of a shared Vision statement. She appoints a Task Force to develop such a Vision. After two months she reviews their work and realizes that they are still developing strategic plans.

Initial Vision statement elements
Work as a team to accomplish key priorities. Perform assessments to ensure efficiencies. Obtain feedback from users to provide effective services. Collaborate with other campus units to satisfy campus information needs.

What has been misunderstood? How can she help them better understand what she is hoping to create? Why is this Vision document important?

To a large extent, the confusion is the result of unfamiliarity with the purpose of a Vision document, and the unfamiliar desire of the new Director to involve all staff in direction-setting and decision-making. When combined with a lack of previous creative and participatory management practices, this leads to a continuing failure to recognize the power of organizational aspirations. This organization had envisioned the driving force of organizational growth as a leadership responsibility, with the staff providing supporting efforts such as designing specific and previously determined desired services, service expectations, and measurable objectives. The necessity and benefit of promoting abstract thinking with inspirational materials was foreign to those who have experienced very little shared leadership and governance. A powerful motivational mindset had not been previously promoted or utilized and the concept of group involvement and responsibility for moving forward was not assumed or even entertained. The resulting Vision document reflected these historical assumptions and understandings. It is now time to redefine the underlying expectations for leadership, governance, and performance expectations.

Many organizations make no distinction between their Vision and their Mission. Often there are no Vision documents at all; an organization simply strives to support its Mission through maintaining effective operations. Even when a Vision statement does exist, there are frequently few aspirational aspects, which means that there will be little striving for significantly enhanced service. Many Vision statements simply state that the library strives to provide responsive and proactive service, incorporating state-of-the-art tools and techniques.

A Vision document should speak to desired outputs and impacts compared to other exemplar organizations. It should offer moving targets and great hopes, not obtainable measures. It should provide inspiration to all staff to reach for better types of services, to develop greater impacts for the organization, and to measure up to other leading libraries. It should resonate with staff as a call to service, and it should generate pride in the hopes and efforts of the library. The mantra should be easy enough to remember, and strong enough in terms of motivation to inspire conversations about constant evaluations and to stimulate creative thoughts and actions that might lead to transformational enhancements.

This is very different than a Mission statement, a clearly written document which does not stimulate, but instead explains to users and stakeholders key priorities and provides measurable service expectations for key deliverables. A Mission statement should also serve as the basis for staff-stakeholder conversations that then generate operating goals which describe to internal staff the priority tasks, allow for appropriate resource allocations, and provide measurable objectives for specific tasks and individual assignments that accomplish the stated service deliverables.

Vision documents call for big actions, blue-sky brainstorming, outside-the-box thinking, cross-unit collaborations, and fearless comparisons to other organizations. They accentuate the desire to move forward through constant comparisons to the best existing services and leading service models. They demand explorations and a commitment to improvements.

In many cases, such holistic activities can conflict with traditional unit-based operational evaluations, and their initial implementation may create confusion and discomfort for those comfortable with the status quo. However, over time such cross-unit and organization-wide collaborations often result in new services and opportunities. The public Vision statement supports the new model of participatory decision making, and allows staff to feel safe when suggesting new approaches.

Inspiring Vision statement elements
Be the leading information organization on campus, and serve as a resource for all local and regional information gathering, handling and sharing activities. Develop new tools and techniques that improve our users' information-sharing skills. Collaborate with stakeholders, users, and other campus units to identify new processes and services to address unmet campus information needs. Provide workshops for other campus information and knowledge groups. Work as a team to identify and implement best practices from aspirational institutions. Provide continuous

service quality reviews of all operations that result in exceptional services.

In one specific implementation of aggressively adopting a leading edge service – the acceptance of electronic theses and dissertations (ETD) – the university created a significantly revised service; one in which materials were immediately accessible, fully searchable, better described, stored in a trusted repository, and less expensive for all parties. The Vision-driven emphasis on proactive, collaborative, and exploratory efforts moved this enhancement along when there was no other impetus for such a radical (and ultimately beneficial) result. Vision documents create a climate in which improvements are considered as a natural occurrence, and an organization gains both enhanced services and supported and empowered staff.

In the following case you will observe how responsiveness to user desires is the most important driver of resource reallocation. Identifying the key influencers and addressing their immediate needs is a first priority. Creating an aware staff is a key requirement for improving services. Creating an informed group of stakeholders allows you to develop the most appropriate services that align with their priorities and to reallocate resources by dropping less utilized operations.

Case Study 2: Share and assimilate Mission/ objectives in relation to resources

Your library has been informed by a newly installed corporate administration that it must become more responsive to unmet user needs while also absorbing a significant reduction in resources. How does your library create new strategic objectives? How does your library begin to modify priorities, develop reasonable service goals, and satisfy user expectations for new services with fewer resources at your disposal?

The first message you have received and need to take action upon is that you will have reduced resources in the future. You will be forced to reconsider your services and modify your operations. Hopefully you already have some ideas of where opportunities exist for discovering savings while minimizing the negative impact upon your users. This news is neither surprising nor tragic for a prepared organization.

The second, and more immediately important, realization is that there is obvious and vocal dissatisfaction expressed by your users to upper management. This is never how you should learn of internal problems, and such scenarios only make your upper management less confident in your abilities to provide appropriate and effective services. It is no surprise that you are not provided with additional resources at this time. This situation could have been avoided if you had regular feedback mechanisms in place to measure user satisfaction. Appearing unaware and then reactive is far less impressive than being sensitive and proactive to changing user needs and desires.

The immediate concern you must address is where are your priorities and the expectations of your users not in alignment? Do you have strategic plans and documented priorities? Have these priorities been recently reviewed, and have you included your users in these decisions? If yes, perhaps you do not have effective and representative members of your feedback groups. If not, it is now time to include your users and their expectations in your planning efforts.

Another immediate concern you must address is how well are the newly discovered and unmet user expectations aligned with your current operations? Can you quickly modify your existing operations to accommodate these high priority services? Is it possible to quickly reallocate support by postponing or dropping less important services in order to assume these more important tasks? Of course you will later perform more systematic reviews in order to develop the most efficient and effective operations, but for now it is more important to demonstrate flexibility and agility rather than efficiency.

Once you have addressed the most immediate concerns, it is time to involve your entire staff in a process that will explore and clarify the intentions, the available resources, the strategic priorities, the measurable goals, and the responsibilities of all within the library in moving toward and ensuring that the library remains a more responsive service operation. This is a long-term process that will require significant participation of all staff in a series of all-staff meetings. Actions and reviews of successful implementations that are initiated as the result of these meetings will be managed by a mix of short term project groups and continuing service review committees. While it is essential to involve all staff in these deliberations in order to develop a shared perspective on the Mission and the priorities, it is equally important for your key stakeholders to feel involved and informed.

Library users and key stakeholders must be brought into the process once the library is a united organization that is ready to speak with one voice about possibilities and the trade-offs that must be made under limited resource conditions. Presenting a set of additional options, which are uncovered during environmental scans for best practices, will create more informed stakeholders. These important advocates and critics will then be better able to identify and weigh previously unrecognized services against known and unsupported needs. Users will also be able to rank all these possibilities against the currently offered services, which will create a set of more user-oriented services and identify areas of less importance to target for the release and reallocation of precious resources.

To accomplish this meeting of the minds and generation of shared priorities the following steps should be followed.

Retreat number one should be an all-library staff event focused on staff education. The emphasis and deliverables should be the creation of a shared vocabulary and a shared understanding of the pressures, the intentions, the timelines, and the resources available to meet any final measurable target services. This is not the time to develop solutions; it is a time to prepare for developing solutions by clarifying understandings, developing buy-in, answering questions about the process, and easing any natural tensions about job loss and learning new tasks. Follow-up sessions for this phase of self-reflection might include training in discovering best practices, evaluation methods, and project management skills. Staff can also start to describe internal resources and existing service review materials. This is also a good time to perform environmental scans to discover important outside trends and aspirational libraries.

Retreat number two occurs when you are coordinated in your actions and ready to invite, educate, and involve your outside users and key stakeholders. Again, you are not yet trying to develop solutions; your intention is to clarify terminology, describe resources, and present options and possible goals. At the end of this session you will perform an initial colored dots exercise to identify initial shared priorities. Your follow-up implementation explorations may determine that the estimated resource requirements necessary to provide these services were underestimated and a reconsideration of priorities might be in order. Be prepared to maintain regular periodic feedback sessions with your users and stakeholders throughout this process to keep them apprised of progress and to respond to any unexpected delays or barriers. Remember that these sessions are just the beginning of an ongoing relationship; you will also maintain regular periodic feedback sessions with your users and stakeholders after the completion of the revisions to be sure you remain responsive to their changing needs.

Retreat number three will be an all-staff meeting to finalize and launch the project management teams that are charged to address the implementation explorations as determined at retreat number two. Once again, you are not yet trying to develop solutions; your intention is to define the domain for each investigation, determine the appropriate members, and describe the process to be used to evaluate local conditions and discover appropriate best practices found within other organizations.

After these three phases are complete you are positioned to start the real work of aligning your new Mission-oriented and user-oriented goals with your remaining resources. This is a task that will require the focused efforts of the project management teams and the episodic attention of others throughout the library and beyond as implementation issues arise.

At this time, and not before, it is appropriate to engage the administrative and operational hierarchy in order to monitor the overall progress of the many active teams. With the benefit of a library-wide perspective, these administrative groups are in a position to quickly recognize potential downstream problems when the progress reports are delivered. If they determine that the collective resource requests are beyond expectations they can alert all involved that it is time to reconsider the initial priorities and resource allocations. They can also address requests for additional support by the individual teams, after obtaining appropriate feedback from the users and stakeholders. In this way a balanced plan is maintained that addresses the top priorities, aligns services with reduced budgets, and prepares the organization for future collaborations, evaluations, and timely service revisions.

While the administration can take the blame for poor performance, only the entire staff, working closely with the users and key stakeholders, should take credit for effectively aligning the library Mission and available resources with user priorities.

That is why the administration should promote creativity awards for staff enhancement ideas and improvements, as well as advocacy awards to recognize user contributions and deeply involved stakeholders.

Decide on transitional or transformative change

Determine at the outset if the end-product of your required review is limited to a re-engineering of existing operations or if you are willing to engage in a far more comprehensive Service Quality Improvement analysis that might significantly change the organization if that is determined to be the most beneficial outcome. Success can be subtle or significant, depending upon how your organization already compares to best practices and the level of your organization's administrative commitment to embracing Service Quality Improvement (SQI) procedures. These driving decisions on ultimate objectives can be difficult to communicate, especially if you are just becoming a high performing organization and staff are not comfortable with possibly radical changes to organizational operations, priorities, and job responsibilities. In other cases, the staff may desire more significant changes than the organization is ready to consider, and frustrations may build.

Once these key objective decisions are made, it is important to share the final objectives and involve the entire staff in early discussions of intentions and possible limitations to review elements. Staff with a clear understanding of the parameters of the review and the potential impacts of changes will be much more willing to participate in brainstorming sessions. The deep knowledge only held by those performing current operations is vital to a thorough and successful review, and this should be made clear and demonstrated at the outset of any review process.

Emphasize an ongoing process

It is also important to remind all staff that any specific review is part of a larger organizational process. The organization will be undergoing multiple concurrent reviews looking for avenues for improvement, utilizing a variety of techniques, communicating lessons learned over time, and developing more mature methods of reviewing operations. Staff should expect the organization to incorporate continuous feedback mechanisms after completion of modifications as a means to regularly monitor and further improve the productivity of all aspects of the entire operation.

In the following case you will see how the strategic plan for a unit drives both the priorities and continual modifications to operations. This underlying vision then results in measurable objectives and an associated budget request with clear justifications that address both unit-specific and library-wide implications and priorities.

Case Study 3: Binding program plan creation

A recently hired Library Director is attempting to understand her new organization, and her first discovery is that there is no detailed budget for the library. Units and services do not appear to have matched clearly defined tasks with associated budgets. Instead there is only historical spending information, with no program plans, no requests for new monies, no documentation of productivity and effectiveness over time, nor any justifications for historical modifications to allocations. The best summary that can be pulled together includes unit annual allocations, expenditures, and quantitative statistics. There appears to be no documentation of any competition for resources among the library units.

Given this scenario, a request for a continuation of an annual $60,000 supplement to an existing $40,000 budgeted Binding Services allocation arrives in her office for its usual approval. Not surprisingly, the Director asks for some background for such an allocation methodology, and asks for the implications if the entire supplement amount is not approved.

The response she receives is that it is not possible to determine the exact impact, as there is no historical breakdown of tasks and expenditures that could be used to make such a projection. It appears that all expenses were recorded as one task, and it was not possible to break out the annual expenditures by project.

The Director calls in the head of collection development, who monitors all Bindery budgets, and asks for as much detail as possible from various invoices. The head of Binding is asked to make best guess estimates about the historical percentages of the budget that were dedicated to various tasks such as journal binding, monograph binding, special monograph binding projects, rebinding for circulation problems, stacks conservation and preservation projects, maps conservation, and any other known initiatives. The head of Binding and the head of Collection Development, with the assistance of the head of Serials Cataloging, are tasked to describe the reduction in the receipt and binding of paper journals over that period. As e-books were just starting to be ordered, the reduction in paper monograph orders would not significantly influence the binding figures to be analyzed.

The head of Binding is also asked to create a zero-based budget for current operations, using standard costs for a local bindery. These same figures are to be used to show calculated costs over the past eight years, given the number and types of materials that were processed according to the reviewed invoices. At the end of this process, undetermined expenditures are to be placed in a budget category entitled Unknown.

The head of Binding is then asked to create a program plan, with clearly defined objectives and priorities. The plan is to describe the present levels of support in terms of relative priorities and underlying program goals. The head of Binding is then asked to describe the implications and propose how reduced allocations would be utilized in the future, starting with only the original $40,000 allocation and rising up through the full $100,000 historical allocation. All involved are told not to make comparisons to past service levels or results, but instead to concentrate on what can be accomplished through either continuing existing operations and/or implementing radically different approaches.

Finally, there is to be an attempt to provide justifications for any changing emphases that were observed over time. There is no need to assign responsibility for the decisions, but merely to document the logic behind the historical trends. The Director hopes this speculative information might be useful in documenting the way the previous administration balanced competitive claims across organizational units.

Needless to say, the total review resulted in some unusual observations, especially in the reassignment of prior journal binding monies into other operations and tasks, without any organizational competition for these released funds for other priorities. Other library administrators were unaware of the budget details and special projects that were funded, and while many of these initiatives were determined to be worthwhile, they would not have been given as high a priority as other services that were allocated inadequate funds or none at all.

As a result of this analysis a program plan was created with justifications for levels of service, measurable objectives for evaluating the services, and a studied decision was made on the appropriate associated funding allocations. Certain services were reduced, others were postponed or dropped, and additional allocations were re-directed toward other library priorities. Similar program plans and budget justifications were then created for other library services and units. It took a while, but there were eventually underlying justifications and measurable objectives for each service, and various operations were modified based upon user needs and revised operations, releasing certain historically repeating funds for new and enhanced services.

Continue to communicate your clear intentions

Communication involves two-way participation, so a regular feedback mechanism such as a web site for current updates and question and answer (Q&A) responses is a key to keeping staff engaged.

As organizations are frequently performing numerous reviews at the same time, it is important to clearly and consistently articulate the various objectives and the progress on each project to avoid generating confusion, conflicts, and inefficiencies. It is well worth taking time to clearly document and communicate intentions rather than attempt to revise mis-informed or mis-directed staff efforts once a process is mis-represented.

Staff should be shown how each specific review is aligned with the organization's highest priorities; progresses by continuing the practice of identifying and adopting best industry practices, and results in implementing new and desirable trends and user services. All employees and users should be able to recognize that in its totality the review and enhancement process is a sound investment. They should be able to communicate the message that change is inevitable, and that the administration is using a well-conceived analytic method in tough times to effectively drop certain historical tasks. Finally, every staff member should be able to explain how this approach benefits the entire organization, all the staff, and the end users.

Managing operations or managing expectations

Success in performing Service Quality Reviews involves more than just staff interaction and involvement leading to revised operations. Most libraries are ultimately service organizations, and are at least partly evaluated through satisfaction measures of their users. Therefore, it is essential to consider the importance of stakeholder involvement and advocacy when determining goals, designing new processes and objectives, and demonstrating effectiveness.

It is not enough to show you are doing things efficiently, you must demonstrate effectiveness. If you are not seen as responsive and aware of stakeholder needs you will be vulnerable to resource cuts when times get tough and priorities are set by those unfamiliar with your efforts and services. Testimonials of significant impact through the design and management of sensitive and appropriate services are a key element in obtaining and retaining fiscal support. Informed stakeholders – those in powerful decision-making positions within your organization – should be integrated into designing your suite of information services, and should provide continuous feedback on current and desired service priorities. A satisfied and forward thinking client, with high expectations for your ability to generate new and responsive services, is your best spokesperson.

Many library budget request presentations focus on how efficiently operations are running; the supposedly persuasive argument often highlights internal operations with little meaning or feeling from those making decisions of vital import to the entire organization. While you want to display ways in which you are providing ever more efficient operations, be sure to focus the majority of your presentation and requests on services with timely "perceived" values.

Consider the possibility that difficult financial times may provide the opportune time to concentrate on a priority of secondary importance for readers and scholars, but of high priority for administrators looking to demonstrate Return on Investment (ROI). Relationships developed over time through providing sensitive, creative and surprising types of information support will often generate long-term benefits in unexpected ways. Be seen as a problem solver in your organization and you will be trusted as an agent for change within your own operation.

The following case will demonstrate the importance of having clear intentions and expectations before embarking upon a new project. The lesson learned is the importance of involving actual users and obtaining user feedback in advance of any actions in order to understand key local considerations. Libraries often see unexpected benefits from early user participation in explorations, experience immediate adoption of new services, and see far-reaching positive ramifications of presenting well-designed services, both within the library and from outside stakeholders.

Case Study 4: Feedback methods important for enhancements and testimonials

The library is approached by a member of the instructional technology unit within the larger organization, and is asked if they are interested in collaborating on an exploration of newly discovered collaboration equipment. The described equipment is new to the organization, relatively untested in similar organizations, and quite expensive. While the exploration may not result in a practical service improvement, it will at least offer an opportunity to develop a stronger relationship with this other information unit that might lead to future service enhancements. The library agrees to explore the possibilities.

The equipment under investigation is a table with networked connections that will allow laptops or mobile devices to display their screens onto a large shared LCD (liquid crystal display) screen. The novelty is in the ease with which the display functions; it is a simple plug-and-play mechanism with a single button to switch the display to a particular device. The equipment functions with most computers and mobile devices, although there are special adapters that are required for certain non-standard connectors. The video demonstration provided by the company seems impressive. The exploration team can imagine this tool will facilitate many types of group work, both for real-time teaching and in supporting group study sessions.

The team decides that it is time to institute a two-pronged approach: exploring the technology itself and understanding the unique and desirable options presented by the technology.

The group performs experiments on a demonstration table at a local corporation during a trial implementation. They learn a good deal about the functionality, the ergonomics, and the potential improvements that could be made for what they believe will be their particular population needs. After some creative building, they are able to create similar collaboration tables with even better capabilities for a significantly less expensive per table price. This flexibility and creative development are distinct advantages of having an in-house technology staff.

In terms of understanding the possibilities and desirability of such a collaboration tool, the team decided to conduct feedback sessions with potential users through the two regular library advisory councils and the use of ad hoc focus groups. The outline of these sessions was to (1) describe and demonstrate the already known possibilities, then (2) ask users for their impressions of these options, plus (3) ask for any other uses that were not already mentioned.

The feedback sessions were informative in unexpected ways. The team was surprised that some users were not as immediately impressed or excited about the possibilities during initial conversations, but the demonstration always created great interest. This taught us not to rely on conversations or storyboards when attempting to measure excitement levels – only actual demonstrations created the impacts and allowed us to register the real interest of user populations. While some people are good at visualizing end-products from concepts, most people require demonstrations for meaningful comprehension.

As expected, through the feedback sessions we learned of new possibilities for the technology that we had not even considered. Some of these were directly related to complicated pedagogy requirements, and others were in relation to addressing nuances that were advantageous for facilitating smoother dynamic aspects of group collaboration, data sharing and project reviews.

In this feedback process expectations were explained, enhancements to existing tools and techniques were demonstrated, and simple instructions were created for public posting. As a result of this proactive stakeholder interaction, users adopted the new collaboration workstations immediately – without the need for any training. In a matter of days our new tool became essential and paradigm shifting. Within weeks we had requests for additional collaboration tables on other floors, and teaching departments were contacting the instructional technology unit about creating collaboration tables for their buildings.

Testimonials from students and teachers continued to pour in at our strategically placed comment boxes. It was clear that our collaboration equipment had modified study behaviors for students, and was having an impact on future pedagogy through conversations with specific "early adopter" teaching faculty. We began discussing another potential paradigm-shifting instruction tool with some of these early adopters – an interactive table which projected a normal computer screen onto a large table-top – and also incorporated collaboration and smart board capabilities. This interactive table became the favorite tool of a particular chemistry professor for its ability to facilitate group viewing of crystal structures, and he eventually decided to hold his office/contact hours in the library. This development also had unintended benefits, as this library-based experience raised his awareness of the increase in library use and the new types of group study activities that were occurring. The experience also allowed him to witness the advantage of using conference tables for better group interactions and dynamics. This professor is now a great advocate for the library.

As expected, word of this tool also reached other teaching faculty, and the Center for Teaching and Learning staff came to the library to better understand the tools we were providing in the library. They are now including these tools in their teacher training, and we have again seen a request for these types of tools across the entire organization. In addition to having our exploratory tools adopted by others, we now have an even better relationship with the organization that addresses pedagogy modifications, which positions us for even deeper integration into curriculum support efforts.

Two recent visits by members of the state-wide Executive Board included demonstrations of these tools, and stories of their adoption by various units throughout our organization. The promotion of these novel tools and the cutting-edge experiences they offered were highlights of their visits that were mentioned at later Board meetings. We created two additional important stakeholder advocates.

This willingness to explore possibilities with others, combined with appropriate interactions with our users early in the process to understand their needs and desires, resulted in unquestionable success and tremendous positive impacts. This type of success created advocates who are excited by our efforts, and this may result in our receiving additional funds to continue pushing the envelope – perhaps into our next investigations of projection systems for news broadcasts and other displays of other types of data using touch screens in auditorium settings for immersion possibilities.

The preceding Cases have demonstrated that it is essential for all staff and users to understand the underlying intentions of each review initiative. Are conditions right for a modest re-engineering in order to find savings or is it an opportune time to explore significant transformations that may provide both savings and enhanced services? Perhaps it is only time to revise operations to uncover savings in order to re-purpose resources toward higher priorities. The desired intentions set realistic expectations and define the scale of the review itself.

Regardless of the financial or other driving influences that generate specific reviews, it is important to provide ongoing service reviews, and to involve users and stakeholders in these analyses. Ensuring that user-oriented perspectives are the focus, and that stakeholder expectations are an important part of early explorations, will guarantee that your initial actions will address the important service issues. The inclusion of all staff and users in deeper analyses will result in strategic plans that best align your resources with Mission priorities and appropriate user needs. Such inclusive exploration teams will also result in more developed staff skills, improved inter-library communications, and stronger stakeholder relationships.

3

A few important analysis techniques

Abstract: An organization requires a suite of analysis tools and techniques in order to remain flexible and agile. Part of this suite are methods and tools used to offer a wide range of qualitative and quantitative measures and analyses. Equally important is a well-prepared and trained staff who know how to identify and evaluate services. Attitude and aptitude are equally prized by good managers, and never more so than under challenging fiscal pressures which create added and distracting tensions. Using the right tools the correct way will keep an organization focused on devising the best solutions to the relevant and manageable targets. A few key techniques are Project Management for coordinating efforts, Interest Based Problem Solving for uncovering hidden causal factors, and Service Quality Improvement for creating a culture of continuous reviews and environmental scanning for best practices.

Key words: analysis, tools, techniques, data, project management, Interest Based Problem Solving, Service Quality Improvement, environmental scans, best practices, benchmarks, standards.

Reviewing operations proactively and willingly

Due to changing internal conditions or outside influences you will occasionally be faced with fixing a perceived problem. A manager can either wait for such needed reviews to arise and perform independent service reviews while under time pressures, or provide a structure and a toolkit of techniques for reviewing and revising operations on a regular basis according to a plan that demonstrates careful consideration. Well-designed analysis includes methods to evaluate situations, identify options, plan for retooling operations, monitor expected progress and predicted results, and adjust plans addressing inevitable unexpected conditions all the way through to completion.

In difficult financial times you will be required to review and revise operations, regardless of whether your organization is functioning well or not. The same analysis tools and techniques are required as mentioned above, but there may be different priorities and intentions driving the solutions.

To reduce the possible repetition of a crisis management scenario, it is best to include steps to measure your organization's performance following a modification. Even if the modification is unplanned and is a result of normal operations, documenting the lessons learned during a service review and revision is a great way to both build staff expertise in following best workflows and to develop a guide for choosing the best methods for a particular type of problem. Develop an adventurous organizational attitude that willingly accepts risks and recognizes the benefits of lessons learned from unexpected outcomes during less than completely successful revision operations. Understand that some experiments will not result in perfect solutions, and that no revision is irreversible if the trial result is less than the intended outcome. Assessments, analyses, enhancements, and reconsiderations are now expected parts of responsible management practices.

Analyses can be small or grand in scope, and can result in incremental or transformational changes. There may be many options available at any one time, but specific times call for the selection of one method among many. If you have a large array of tools and appropriately trained personnel at your disposal you can utilize the right method at the right time, making your efforts most appropriate and advantageous.

Beyond re-engineering

Re-engineering is often seen by managers as a powerful method of revising operations in order to obtain efficiencies. Such re-engineering is often made possible due to new automation or new processes. Alert managers always look for new tools and techniques to improve operations. Environmental scans of peer operations and the industry in general discover best practices and consortial solutions that either reduce costs and/or enhance operations. Incorporating revisions into current operations is now expected, and making consolidations and reductions in services during tough times is an easy way to demonstrate appropriate management oversight and creativity through re-engineering efforts.

Successful outcomes of such re-engineering efforts and more efficient staff practices with the associated recovery or re-purposing of discovered savings are common. While re-engineering does improve operational efficiencies and recovers staff time and financial resources for supporting new services, it often involves only a small modification and a small recovery of resources. In certain circumstances a proactive and aware manager can recognize that larger modifications could be made and larger savings could be gained through a more intensive process utilizing alternative and more comprehensive organizational review options. Creative managers look for opportunities for significant transformational changes and associated savings rather than settling for easily found transitional modifications and incremental savings.

As financial resources shrink, administrators expect managers to reduce costs through creative and sometimes painful reductions in operating costs. This reallocation of resources among services may involve reducing services or service quality. Transformational changes may allow for reallocating limited resources more toward where they are perceived as most important, while reducing support where services are no longer as desired. Especially when services are reduced in importance, there may be very different and less expensive ways to obtain adequate results, with less resource allocation, than using the originally designed methods.

The importance of project management

Regardless of whether a process is being significantly or minimally modified, the most effective way to ensure an adequate result is to utilize a well-designed Project Management plan. Implementing a formal project management process ensures that groups address such important aspects of the methodology as defining the problem, identifying the possible solutions, coordination, collaboration, participation, monitoring, reporting progress and requesting additional resources, and completing the modifications while meeting the original outcomes. Maintaining adequate attention to all these simultaneous considerations requires both training and a supporting infrastructure.

There are a number of tools developed to describe and assist groups in undertaking the steps involved in these complex project management operations. While organizational training will develop a larger group of mature project managers, it is helpful to use these project management documentation tools to guide teams through a successful project.

In the following case one can observe how exploring the effectiveness of an existing operation can lead to both improvements in current operations and entirely new services. In this case, a project to review and revise current e-book support led to significant modifications to existing policies and procedures and to recovered savings for expanded services. The key to such flexibility is a library-wide perspective that emphasizes the why rather than the what of operations.

Case Study 5: E-book explorations lead to new processes and policies

Most libraries had their entrance into the e-book realm through exploring e-reference packages. These initial e-book purchases and leases were the result of obtaining pre-selected packages of online reference books that were thought to be far more useful for people in remote settings where they would normally have the need for quick facts. Very few early e-book purchases were initiated by individual user requests. Ironically, while the costs for e-reference tools are often far higher than for their paper counterparts due to annual fees that support enhanced functionality and more frequent updates, there have been very few evidence based analyses of the effectiveness of these tools. Anecdotal evidence seems to indicate that many of these tools are not used as often as initially expected, be that because they are not easily and seamlessly searched or due to more popular free online tools that may be less authoritative but are adequate for many users.

Over time the growth and adoption of fulltext journals plus the success of e-readers generated a market for e-books. Public libraries quickly adopted the readers and are actively working with publishers and book vendors to develop best practices that satisfy user demands and provide reasonable revenue for authors and publishers. Larger corporate and academic libraries also expanded into single e-book orders as newer reference titles were required on additional platforms. This was especially true for niche encyclopedias and handbooks. This support for alternative platforms and one-off purchases required the development of more sophisticated policies and procedures for selection and acquisition.

The most adventurous designers in the library community began by first scanning for all available options and systematically identifying preferred and required functionalities. They then created a matrix for recording and ranking criteria when options existed on multiple platforms. Some of the considerations included pricing, interface options, bibliographic record quality and ease of batch loading, and technical capabilities to seamlessly electronically exchange orders and funds. Another key criterion was the ability to integrate their services with existing paper book vendors in order to minimize overlaps in notification slips and to avoid duplicate purchases with paper orders through existing approval plans or from selector firm orders.

It was a short step from selecting individual reference books to expanded selection and acquisition of stand-alone monographic e-books and e-book series. Many questions still remained within the libraries, such as: Would the library always be supporting both formats and how equally would parallel paper or e-book ordering be supported in the future? How long of a lag time would be acceptable before the library initiated automatic orders of paper versions? Would these decisions be the same for all disciplines and all publishers according to current approval plan criteria? Would libraries want to duplicate the current paper approval plan as the basis of an e-book approval plan and/or notification plan? Would libraries need to create new approval plan profiles, and could/should they utilize the same approval plan vendor for e-books and paper books?

In addition to developing an infrastructure that supported many types of individual e-book acquisitions, libraries decided to explore user adoption and behavior using a larger aggregated package of titles. At the time only Academic Complete from ebrary offered such a broad collection of titles across many disciplines, so we initiated a trial, knowing we would need to work with multiple vendors to address overlap and duplicate order concerns. We also had concerns about dedicating significant dollars to a just-in-case package of e-books when we were already reducing our monograph firm order funds to dangerously low levels in order to maintain journal subscriptions with high inflation rates. We decided to treat the e-book package as an exploration for one year to allow us to observe use patterns and determine satisfaction and scalable support needs. We recognized that if we canceled the package we might need to purchase some heavy-use titles from another platform. We decided to take this risk and perhaps double purchase some titles if necessary in order to better understand our local user needs and preferences through actual experiences rather than through relying upon anecdotal comments and literature reviews that described a relatively small body of general e-book use.

The discussion of just-in-case purchasing of e-books through a package next lead us to wonder why we maintain an automatic approval plan for e-books when we can have immediate and seamless access on demand using patron-driven acquisitions (PDA) for e-books? Perhaps we could even use PDA for paper books if we were willing to accept the slight delay for physical delivery, which is dropping to one day thanks to faster and more reasonable printing and shipping options. Based upon our previous work with our e-book plaforms and our book vendors, we instituted a PDA trial of record delivery, seamless ordering, duplicate removal for our other vendor plans, and electronic payment. The initial design and implementation of the complicated integrated processes started a bit rough, but eventually proved viable. The library is now expanding from a trial to a regular PDA record load based in large part on our present paper book approval and notification plan. This migration was made after investigation showed a 3:1 ratio of use between our firm orders and automatic profile selections. Other libraries have found similar ROI benefits from PDA experiences. By moving more toward PDA rather than automatic ordering we will save money, build a more responsive delivery system, and be able to re-dedicate some of our savings to a broader base of available titles.

The advances and advantages just described are limited to our own users, as e-book sharing and interlibrary loan policies are not yet widely available. Ironically, as more members of our formal and informal consortia adopt e-books we lose access to large segments of collections that are no longer sharable. Until consortia, book publishers, and vendors work together to develop pricing models for shared materials we are actually reducing our access to materials by nature of their format. This is a situation that requires collaboration and compromise in order to develop a system that provides easy access to the largest possible set of materials while still preserving the required peer review, copy editing, and advanced navigation and distribution networks that users expect. Such consortial solutions will challenge designers due to the complex profiles required for handling central budgeting of unpredictable purchases and automatic selections of multiple options based upon local preferences. The cooperating libraries themselves must develop best practices for addressing duplicate paper considerations, balancing repurposed savings toward other priorities or back into collections for expanded coverage of shared e-books beyond the core materials, and appropriate balances of just-in-case purchases for core materials and PDA for esoteric materials. Another policy decision that must be considered is will libraries with e-book titles be allowed to raid other libraries for paper copies? This is a phenomenon that has been seen, but perhaps as users become more comfortable with the advantages of e-books they will modify their preference for paper books in many situations. Then again, it may be interlibrary loans of paper titles will always be an option for certain types of uses, and we may modify our profiles for e-books to reflect these circumstances.

What we have seen here is a continual shift in operating procedures and services as technologies mature and we understand how to maximize the new options. We went from creating and updating an e-book ordering process through new paradigms for e-book packages and on-demand ordering, and eventually to collaborating with other libraries and publishers to develop shared purchasing options that will improve functionality and broaden access at reduced prices.

These advances are possible because libraries are able to work across units, with users, and with systems developers to explore options, test possibilities, and revise and devise processes and policies that continually expand and influence the development of new services.

Problem discovery processes

Project management is not a method used only for initiating new efforts. The methodology is important and valuable for monitoring and facilitating any ongoing operation that requires careful oversight. Even periodic service reviews can benefit from utilizing a project management framework.

All libraries should perform continual reviews of their services and their service effectiveness. LibQUAL+ and other tools can provide a framework for a project management plan that includes important baseline data and a feedback mechanism for updated reviews of certain service areas over time. There are many other standard library assessment practices published that include best practices for measuring effectiveness against industry benchmarks. ARL SPEC Kits are an excellent source of such guidelines. The library literature also includes many project plans for analysis of services. Take advantage of the work done by others to adopt a project plan that has proven effective, rather than developing your own methods from scratch. Of course, you may need to modify these project plans to accommodate local conditions, but the basic steps are still valid and can save you time in identifying best measures, industry benchmarks, problems to avoid, and possible alternative solutions to known conditions.

Initial project management steps include clearly defining the interests, understanding the implications, charting the tasks and dependencies among them, obtaining feedback throughout the process as circumstances change, and requesting additional resources and administrative support if necessary. These steps will lead to a complete and careful evaluation and revision of an existing process or the successful implementation of a new service.

Any proposed project goals should first be compared to the organization's Mission, resources, and priorities. Only library-wide priorities should be supported with appropriate resources, and cross-unit communication and planning are essential for flexible and agile responses. Unit goals should be based upon these organizational priorities, and individual and group SMART (specific, measurable, attainable, realistic and timely) goals should be aligned with these higher level goals. Project management goals and priorities must be both appropriate and significant enough to deserve the resources and ultimately warrant the distraction and disruption that will be caused to normal operations.

In tough financial and staffing circumstances choices must be made, and purposeful abandonment of less essential or outdated tasks must be considered. In addition, remember to celebrate and demonstrate success to both improve staff morale and develop compelling arguments and incentives for additional initiatives.

Evaluation of intention

Before you start to take action on any service reviews you should ask one key question: Why are you performing this assessment?

Assessment can be used for two distinct reasons: either (1) performing Service Quality Improvement initiatives that enhance current operations, or (2) identifying savings through reductions in services. One should consider the desirable outcomes before embarking on gathering data. These two intentions can involve very different variables, and you must be studying the correct variables to discover the best alternatives in the most efficient manner. With a clear purpose in mind, and clear priorities developed with stakeholder contributions, the appropriate statistical data can be collected for meaningful analysis and modifications. Quite often far more data is gathered than is necessary, and often the wrong type of data is gathered to perform powerful analysis leading to better operations.

Identifying the actual problem

Once the intentions are clear in terms of scale of change under consideration, it is time to be certain that the project will be addressing the causal factors driving a need for change, rather than just correcting the symptoms of a hidden underlying condition. Too often managers attempt to modify a problem scenario without first identifying the deeper situations that generate the problem conditions. This may create a quick fix, but it is likely that problems will return or be created in other related areas.

A complete review of a problem scenario will require a well-considered plan, which begins by involving all the relevant personnel in a flowcharting exercise for the current steps in an operation. This will highlight the many complex and often competing processes, interests, and timelines that require attention and detailed review. Often a modification in one small detail of one workflow can create impacts on seemingly unrelated activities. Understanding the relationship among operations will identify areas of mutual concern in terms of associations and reliance.

Once all relationships are documented it is possible to look at the underlying interests and mine deep into operations to identify the conditions that can be modified to provide a better scenario. Finding actual causal factors may require multiple stages of exploration. In some cases the discovery process will require a series of "What is the underlying concern or need?" questions to determine the actual underlying causes or interests. People and organizations develop habits of unintentionally disguising deep interests when dealing with emotional issues. This may come from trust issues or simply a failure to recognize that multiple interests may be operating below the surface. It is often unpleasant to recognize and publicly state concerns that might be rooted in underlying security or adequacy considerations. These difficult issues must be identified if a review is to address the core issues that need to be considered in developing a mutually satisfactory solution to a current problem scenario.

While there are many ways to uncover underlying causes, such as the flowcharting method mentioned above to discover process issues, there is one particular type of cause that requires a specific technique to assist in bringing these conditions to the surface. When dealing with conflicting personnel issues it is often difficult to identify the actual causal factors due to the emotions that mask many under-lying fears. Interest Based Problem Solving techniques are often quite helpful in burrowing beneath the symptoms and identifying the hard to admit concerns on each side of the situation. After some honest guided conversation, it is often possible to easily find many mutual interests which can be removed from deliberation, allowing the parties to concentrate on the few remaining important concerns.

Interest Based Problem Solving

Interest Based Problem Solving (IBPS) is an approach used to uncover underlying causes of contention that may be masked and difficult to determine for a variety of reasons. These exploration methods are used by a group of participants who are experiencing impasse difficulties. The methods facilitate contemplating the actual causal factors involved by reaching back to primary concerns to identify underlying special interest factors. These deeper explorations of the problem scenario, utilizing specific interest-based analysis techniques, often uncover unspoken concerns. The process identifies key decision factors that are not initially evident and therefore not addressed, assisting in recognition and allowing negotiations to occur on important considerations. This interest evaluation results in precise and meaningful action on essential concerns, rather than continuing to spend time working on unsuccessful deliberations that focus on concerns that are merely superficial symptoms of a much deeper issue.

In order for IBPS to succeed, there are a few conditions that must be in place. The required environmental scenario must address both process and content concerns. They fall into two categories – understanding how to work together and creating a clear set of priorities.

Trust

In terms of understanding how to work together, there must be a process that allows for open and honest statements of concern, regardless of the harshness of the truths exposed. The initial conversations will be based upon trust in the process itself, rather than trust in the participants. Over time a relationship will develop which will result in greater comfort with honest declarations of interest. Trust must exist at the start, even if there is not complete transparency.

Especially at the outset, or when new members are introduced and clear behavior guidelines are still becoming natural, it is advantageous to involve a neutral facilitator. This facilitator is not a negotiator, and this person will only step in if/when situations become tense. Their role is to help the participants follow the rules, recognize the underlying concerns, and utilize the best methods to address the discovered concerns. They do not participate in negotiations or speak of the values raised in the meetings.

The goal of the facilitator is to develop an environment that allows for maximum transparency. This generally means that the climate should be one of respect – each person should be provided a fair opportunity to speak, the group must maintain respect for all ideas introduced, all ideas must be allowed to be presented in full before comments are made, and all participants must maintain their calmness and dignity in all situations.

Agenda

In terms of processes that lead to such open conversations, the facilitator may emphasize that the best conversations and deliberations result from a clear agenda and a well-run meeting. Complete and effective agendas clarify each item as to intention (discussion, collaboration, consensus, or an action item that will lead to a vote). Every discussion should begin with the distribution of information well in advance of the meeting, with adequate documentation to serve as background and question points, and plenty of time for pre-meeting data gathering, percolation, and contemplation. There should never be even the impression of forced or rushed decisions. Especially important for IBPS conversations are documentation of relevant policies and procedures, and any existing memoranda of understanding for unique situations. It also helps to remind all participants of the lessons learned in the past by the IBPS group in terms of similar rulings and clarifications about existing policies and procedures. Agendas and preparation can make the difference between contentious situations and empathetic scenarios in which there are clear and calm deliberations about concerns that have been deeply considered in advance.

Documentation

In addition to setting the meeting conditions for maximum productivity, it is important to have a clear understanding of the organization's operating procedures and priorities. These initial conditions should determine the direction of deliberations. If there is a clear Mission, with a documented vision, defined priorities, clearly articulated unit goals, and aligned individual measurable objectives, the ultimate determination of any scenario must support these principles. Actions must also support clearly articulated standards, rules, and best practices.

Quite often there is a claim of unfair treatment or inconsistency in following stated organizational policies and procedures. One important condition to recognize is that for a variety of performance reasons, it is common to have different unit performance measures. Exceptions based upon organizational needs, such as a different vacation or sick leave notification policy for a high volume delivery unit, will lead to a range of individual performance measures and expectations that are misunderstood or completely unknown to most of the staff. These special conditions must be documented in job descriptions in order to address challenges of unfair treatment. Many grievances are the result of such uniformed review scenarios, and instead of becoming helpful feedback opportunities for all involved, they tend to become emotional conflicts. This type of misunderstanding can be easily corrected if the conditions allow for the calm review of the appropriate documentation. Over time existing staff gain a better understanding of the policies and procedures, the reasons behind the special conditions, and a reasonable expectation of the consequences of exception circumstances.

The uncover process

Once you have the conditions in place to provide a balanced and open deliberation it is important to have the right tools to uncover deeply buried concerns. There are a number of methods that can be used, and below two are mentioned: using a tree structure to uncover layered interests and using charting to relate interests with operations.

Tree structures

A very helpful way to visualize and uncover underlying interests within problem scenarios is to use a tree structure to demonstrate and elucidate underlying interests. In this approach the participants draw a branching hierarchy and continue to explore each branch for vested interests, starting with obvious problems caused by simple confusions or misunderstandings, and delving deeper to eventually discover more significant interest-based disagreements or conflicts. What may start as a discussion of unfair practices may eventually become a conversation about the validity of differing performance expectations. What at first may seem to be a problem with training may eventually become a union classification concern. What starts as a discussion about changing an acquisitions procedure may eventually become a discussion about outsourcing. These types of challenges to actual operations often become deliberations about managerial decisions and the long-term directions of the organization. It is surprising how effectively a series of tough "and what is your interest?" questions asked at the right time while exploring scenarios can uncover the actual causes of concern that are not initially recognized or willingly divulged.

For example, staff in acquisitions are being introduced to a new online book ordering tool. There appears to be resistance. After some initial discussion it seems that there is serious concern about learning a new book ordering tool from another vendor.

The resistance is initially presented as the comment: We do not have enough time to learn yet another tool.

The following questions and comments explore the underlying feelings and eventually arrive at a number of deep-seated interests that are contributing to this immediate staunch resistance.

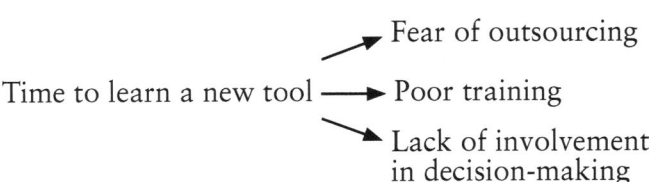

Time to learn a new tool → Fear of outsourcing
Time to learn a new tool → Poor training
Time to learn a new tool → Lack of involvement in decision-making

BRANCH 1

"what is your interest?" Maintaining an adequate productivity level.

Comment: I fear a negative evaluation of my value.

"what is your interest?" Showing productivity and local knowledge.

Comment: Very concerned about not appearing necessary.

"what is your interest?" Demonstrating my worth.

Comment: Showing value of a person with local expertise.

"what is your interest?" Keeping my job.

Comment: Heard of outsourcing for efficiencies.

Actual concern: Don't want to make the new process appear to be more efficient/effective than me. As this will lead to my position being outsourced.

BRANCH 2

"what is your interest?" Appearing to adapt to ever greater numbers of new tools.

Comment: Very concerned about not appearing current and sharp.

"what is your interest?" Having adequate preparation and documentation.

Comment: Fear my training will not be adequate.

"what is your interest?" Not failing or failing due to a poor trainer.

Comment: We are often left to create our own best practices.

"what is your interest?" Protect myself, not covering a poor trainer.

Comment: So many people fear that they are not trained right.

"what is your interest?" Being prepared for a fair evaluation.

Actual concern: Additional inadequate training and a lack of supporting materials about procedures will result in a poor performance report.

BRANCH 3

"what is your interest?" Providing a quick and easy order processing.

Comment: Other new procedures are actually slower than Amazon ordering.

"what is your interest?" Simple, easy, and effective ordering.

Comment: Fear my efforts will be redundant or wasted.

"what is your interest?" Doing the best thing for quick ordering.

Comment: We could create or recognize best practices.

"what is your interest?" Being involved in a best solution.

Comment: People are not asked about changes.

"what is your interest?" Being helpful and respected.

Actual concern: A failure to involve staff performing the day-to-day work in finding the best practices to accomplish their own work.

Some of these explorations will surface legitimate concerns that need to be addressed before any actions are taken, while other avenues of exploration will raise misunderstandings or inaccurate beliefs that must be corrected in order to bring the organization to a place of shared interests, in order to move forward as a team. Be prepared to spend time exploring eventually fruitless paths in order to open conversations that will lead to unexpected paths with significant underlying interests. Expect to discover many branches, and to uncover a number of disturbing problem scenarios that you will be forced to address. These internal problems must be faced and overcome in order to build a better performing organization, a more consistent workplace, and a trust in shared governance.

The key to utilizing this tree branch approach is to concentrate on describing the situation, not solving the problems. The ultimate solution will only appear once the correct conditions are identified. Too often people become distracted and try to correct the situation by addressing the symptoms rather than finding the underlying conditions. It takes perseverance and control to not begin focusing on solving initial problems. To alleviate fears that the initial problems will be forgotten, record each concern by placing each symptom in the parking lot for later consideration if your final solution does not already correct the symptom as a by-product. At most, sketch out possible ways to address the conditions and interests as preliminary approaches, but do not develop solutions. The patterns of concerns you discover as you delve deeper may be useful later, as they may be repeated in other circumstances. Use these as signs of symptoms that lead to more significant interests. Always remain empathetic to all concerns and interests that are raised, but do not start solving problems until you feel certain there are no additional hidden interests remaining.

Your tree structure may become quite intricate and complex, but that is common in an established organization with many layers of operations and interests. Over time you may be able to recognize patterns that cross these interest trees, and that will help you move more quickly along the path to differentiating deeply rooted interests from superficial concerns. What would be quite helpful is a way to overlay these various interest trees in a unified fashion.

Chart goals, operations, and interests

Another excellent way to uncover underlying interests, and to observe the web of associated entanglements that derive from complicated and convoluted relationships between these desires and organizational conditions, is to chart the interests and overlay the organizational goals that are impacted by the culmination of those interests in various manifestations (see Figures 3.1 and 3.2 overleaf). This will allow you to map how the interests of the employees align with the interests of the organization. In some cases all employee interests will align, in other cases there will be different targets, and in some cases the goals of the organization will directly conflict with the interests of some or all employee groups.

One standard type of service charting is done using a Process Flowchart. These charts show initial conditions, questions and result pathways, processes, and feedback loops along the entire life of a service. They often will show dotted lines to impacts on other service operations.

Once you have charted all interests, it is time to classify them in terms of levels of difficulty (see Figure 3.2). We will now look at the possible conditions from easiest to most complex to address.

Quite often there are unrealized common interests buried beneath superficial differences. The recognition of shared priorities and mutually satisfactory solutions that will satisfy all parties makes developing agreements on these conditions quite easy. This success also develops a sense of teamwork that will somewhat ease the forthcoming negotiations.

The next scenario involves related interests, in which it may be possible to uncover not exactly matching priorities, but perhaps parallel interests. Such aligned priorities provide opportunities for compromises that partially satisfy all parties. While providing less than ideal solutions, these

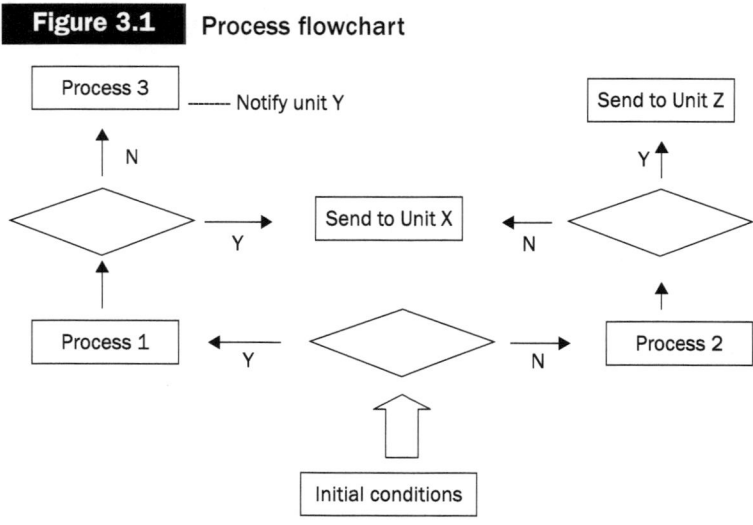

Figure 3.1 Process flowchart

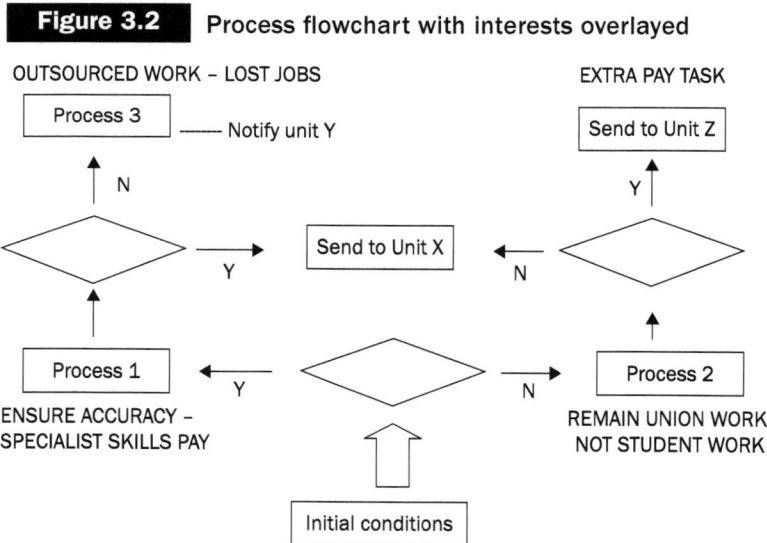

Figure 3.2 Process flowchart with interests overlayed

compromises can generate immediate understandings, comfort in negotiations, and perhaps even trust that will lead to a deeper willingness to work together in the future toward additional compromises.

Most difficult situations are the result of significant and competing interests. Identify the deepest concerns of both parties and attempt to develop balanced settlements. Be reasonable in negotiating; no party wins every demand. Overall, expect to win on certain issues and make concessions in other areas. The most difficult consequence of such reasonable compromises is actually a growing distrust within the represented populations, as each group believes that their negotiators were not effective in making powerful cases. Few outside parties can understand and empathize with the full range of concerns stated at the table, and good leaders must know how to convince their followers of the legitimacy of competing interests. Over time, when making unpopular compromises, trust is as important *within* the special interest populations as it is across the negotiating table.

If all other approaches fail, and best-intentioned negotiations reach an impasse, the team should return to a user-oriented perspective, finding a compromise solution that best supports the organization's Mission. If no such compromise can be determined or agreed upon, then the problem situation must be taken to the next (outside) level of facilitators or administrators for adjudication. This approach is never good, and it should be avoided at all costs, as it clearly demonstrates poor communication, an inability to keep user satisfaction as the primary interest, and a failure to develop shared governance and shared responsibility for decision-making. Such a breakdown in cooperation and collaboration leads to the establishment of strict control mechanisms and results in the loss of agility and flexibility, and increased fear and organizational paralysis. In worst case scenarios, the higher-level decision-makers will assume control, and an organization will receive direction from those unaware of the nuances and the complex sets of concerns of the staff that were already having difficulties.

Outside solutions and top-down scenarios rarely lead to smooth and efficient operations. Compromise is always better than capitulation.

Learn to dig down to find the true concerns, the real underlying issues, and the mutual solutions that are easiest to address; therefore leaving more time and energy to focus on the few significant issues that deserve more attention and compromise. Alleviate unnecessary and debilitating negativity, demonstrate the ability to work together, and develop trust and a better culture across all layers of the organization.

In the following case, the utilization of various exploratory techniques allowed staff to empathetically dig deep and discover mutual interests and special interests that were exposed and addressed. The result was more honest and open communication, and the hope of better relationships through shared decision-making in future scenarios.

Case Study 6: Union and administrative grievances – IBPS reductions

The highest level of administrators in an organization became aware of the significant loss of productivity and the enormous costs expended for outside negotiators in addressing the many grievances continually filed within the library. In addition, the union negotiators had reached an impasse in developing new job descriptions that would allow for any modified operations. The existing library culture was overwhelmed by unnecessary or superficial grievance threats and actual submissions, requiring enormous numbers of meetings by all parties with few settlements, and serious tension and distrust across all layers of the organization. The situation across the entire organization had previously reached such a level of dysfunction that there were multiple strikes and work stoppages. The organization had brought in outside facilitators for the recent negotiations and this had resulted in a long-term contract that should have reduced tensions. However, within the library there still existed paralyzing conditions that negatively affected productivity and creativity. The administration decided to engage the same consultants and facilitators to expose the underlying concerns and allow for better understandings and explorations of current conditions which would lead to revised and more efficient operations.

A brief review of the situation by the library staff resulted in the following summaries of conditions. Concerns were raised by union staff about unfair applications of documented rules, and it was believed that there was a failure of the administration to admit that problems existed. The union stated that rules were never consistently enforced, and no corrective action was taken when problematic conditions were uncovered. Trust had completely eroded that any systematic solution would be forthcoming, and the union believed that only grievances were effective in highlighting specific conditions that needed to be corrected.

The administration felt that there was no understanding or recognition by the union about the primacy of operational needs when considering local exceptions and determining any allowances or flexibility for special requests. Job descriptions became ever more specific and very little flexibility was allowed in new posted positions. Greater emphasis was placed on measurable objectives for each position, and in some cases the same position in different locations had very different expectations due to multi-task responsibilities. It became increasingly more difficult to insert any new tasks into a job description without a major audit and months of negotiation.

Under these conditions, new grievances were filed on a regular basis, and established grievance cases often went on for years.

Some cases were never concluded, most eventually required outside facilitators and mediators, animosity was rampant, and the resulting hardball tactics meant that blatant special interests delayed most new initiatives or considerations.

A team composed of representatives from both the library administration and the union was charged by the administration with studying the problems and presenting solutions. After observing the drastically different versions of the problems from both parties, and the lack of agreement on key concerns and solutions, the team decided to utilize the consulting firm to explore Interest Based Problem Solving (IBPS) methods to determine the deep-seated underlying concerns, and to create a better environment for future collaboration.

Facilitated IBPS methods quickly reduced the number of previously unsolvable problem scenarios by uncovering some surprisingly common interests that contributed to the advancement of the Mission of the organization, and were agreed upon and moved off the table. This progress created some hope among the participants. Another round of IBPS identified some related interests that could be addressed through a series of compromises that were acceptable to both sides.

This left the more difficult situations, and a more intensive facilitation process was used to help the group recognize the deeper interests that were not being expressed due to emotional and logistical considerations. These complex scenarios were explored as impersonal interests of the parties, with respect for the positions and the desires on both sides, and compromises to some conditions were found after calm negotiation addressed the best balance of hopes against realistic expectations that served the users and the Mission of the library.

A final set of conflicting interests were uncovered that addressed the ultimate concerns of outsourcing jobs and participatory governance rules. The resolution of these scenarios required training by team members in how to discuss and negotiate in tense circumstances, and also in how to obtain buy-in from their constituents for positions that were seen as not completely satisfactory compared to previous demands.

After a long period of education and conversation, it was determined that one of the most contentious problems was not often created by inconsistency when applying a single set of rules, but rather a misunderstanding about (1) the legitimacy of multiple conditions, and (2) realistic expectations in various units based upon specific service needs. The situation would be partially rectified by having better staff training about how expectations related to quality service requirements, and by providing greater emphasis on special personnel expectations when discussing job responsibilities during the hiring process. It was also recognized that various unit heads and supervisors would require better training in how to address problem scenarios to avoid immediate confrontations.

In terms of outsourcing, it was determined that this would be allowed for lower-level tasks as long as the existing staff were re-trained for higher-level work, and that all staff would accept some form of accountability for reaching measurable objectives in new position responsibilities. This was seen as a win-win situation that provided higher salaries and greater organizational flexibility.

Eventually, a set of compromises were developed that left the team with a better sense of shared understanding, the ability to work together to create a culture of early problem resolution that might reduce the number of future grievances, and would let the library create new job descriptions that would allow for reasonable flexibility while protecting staffing conditions that would satisfactorily cover the most demanding operational needs. There was a noticeable improvement in the relationships and communication between the library administrators and library union representatives. Most significantly, the highest-level administrators were waiting to see reduced numbers of grievances, improved productivity, and creative responses and new services to satisfy user expectations.

Completing the review program

Identifying possible solutions

Having determined the root causes of any problematic situations, it is now time to develop solutions. These possible actions may cover a continuum from simple replacement of certain workflows to complete redesigns of service models. There may even be the outsourcing of tasks to other internal or external operations. And let us not forget the option of dropping the effort entirely if the cost of correction or enhancement is not worth the ultimate benefit of continuing the service.

The determination of an ultimately wise modification relies upon a thorough review of the alternatives before any decision is made. These possibilities are best discovered by performing environmental scans within the library community, and in some cases in outside but related industries. For instance, moving large numbers of book materials may be fairly well accomplished by other libraries, especially those that have undertaken large collection shifts, but perhaps such shifts are even more efficiently performed in book distributor warehouses by companies such as Baker & Taylor and Amazon. Good managers look beyond the obvious places for new ideas and methods that are appropriate. Best practices can be found in unlikely places.

In addition to discovering new methods that immediately improve services, another way to evaluate operational effectiveness is by comparing your organization's current productivity against industry benchmarks or relative standards. It may be that your local conditions make your customized or tailored approach as effective as the best designed alternative operations under different conditions, but only a trial evaluation period can show this type of comparative effectiveness. Remember your goals, and know that in some cases adopting newly discovered best practices may not result in better service, but only in less expensive costs. This is a success worth investigating, but perhaps not worth broadly promoting.

A thorough review of possible alternatives should result in a suite of possible options that should be considered for implementation. Each option will have benefits and costs, and these should be clearly spelled out before comparing the relative values of the opportunities. The inclusion of all staff working in the considered operations will allow for a more productive initial assessment.

Coordination, collaboration, participation

Once you have identified and described the alternatives it is time to evaluate the options. A successful evaluation requires input from all relevant stakeholders. Early involvement and serious engagement by the full range of participants will result in greater understanding of the scenario by all concerned, informed opinions at decision-making time, organization-wide redesigns that result in smooth transitions and no surprises – which builds confidence, willing buy-in by vested employees from different units, heightened staff morale, and a higher performing organization over time through continuous staff development. These types of positive environments and empowered staffs are noticeable within evolved learning organizations.

Greater support from outside administrators and users is evident in such healthy collaborations, even during difficult financial times when cherished services must be removed or reduced. Informed populations of users are more willing to request additional resources for your organization if they believe you are managing as effectively as possible, and that you will maximize the new resources in creative ways. A library, by the nature of its cross-discipline support and user-oriented facilities and services, is one of only a few operations within an organization that can obtain support from across many groups that are already in fierce competition for limited resources. Demonstrations of comprehensive and participatory decision-making are key elements for continuing support.

Monitoring, reporting progress and requesting additional resources

Throughout the review and redesign process it is therefore important to remain in close contact with key constituents, decision-makers, and stakeholders. People once removed from the process want to know that their interests remain a clear priority, and they want to be told that their concerns are being remembered and addressed as follow-up decisions are being made. As long as they are assured that their interests are being considered, they are likely to maintain a minimal and supportive interest in the progress of your projects.

In communicating with stakeholders, it is important to compare actual progress to the original timelines and measurable objectives. Progress reports should review the adequacy of existing resources, mention and consider the potential impact of any disruptive influences, describe possible modifications to timelines and objectives, highlight any unexpected staffing needs, and seek feedback and support on any and all conditions. It is essential to inform and involve key outside stakeholders and decision-makers in the project as it moves toward completion.

Figure 3.3	Gantt chart demonstrating dependencies and time projections

Personnel	Project	task	duration/dependence	time/effort/progress	time/effort/progress	time/effort/progress	time/effort/progress
John A.	Project A	scan a	30 days	July 1-30, 2013			
Jim D.	Project A	gather b	10 days	July 1-10, 2013			
Jill F.	Project A	design c	45 days*b		July 11-Aug 20, 2013		
Carol N.	Project A	test d	20 days*c			Aug 21-Sep 15, 2013	
Paul G.	Project B	scan e	30 days		July 11-Aug 20, 2013		
Ralph T.	Project B	gather f	10 days		July 11-Aug 20, 2013		
Sue R.	Project B	design g	30 days*f			Aug 21-Sep 25, 2013	
Carol N.	Project B	test g	20 days*c*f				Sep 26-Oct 15, 2013

One effective way to document tasks, dependencies, timelines, and progress is to utilize a Gantt chart. This type of chart, shown as Figure 3.3, is a standard tool in most project management packages, including the Microsoft Project software. Two advantages over a simple spreadsheet tool such as Excel are that work effort can be calculated per person and the projected completion dates of all dependent sub-operations will automatically be shifted when delays are recorded.

Keep in mind that as described in the library-specific article by Zhang and Bishop (2005): "MSP 2000 has a moderate learning curve and is not highly intuitive" and "For small projects, learning a project-management program does not necessarily offer huge advantages. Instead it may be more practical and efficient to create an Excel spreadsheet to manage a small project."

Completing the modifications

Many organizations simply end a project when the designed modifications have been put in place. This is not the sign of a successful project; the implementation of new operations and revised workflows is merely the successful step of transitioning your desired operational means toward a larger goal. Remember that your ultimate goal is to demonstrate the attainment of measurable benchmarks in relation to your original intentions and resources. A project is completed when you have evaluated the ability of your modifications to reach these benchmark production and service values, and when you have promoted these local enhancements and/or savings with an understanding of the trade-offs that have been considered and approved. Until you can demonstrate the impact of the modifications, you are merely providing additional progress reports.

Not all modifications will result in improvements or reach the desired measurable goals. There are many reasons why initial plans and designs do not match actual results, and this is not always a failure of a project. If the project forgot to consider some key variables, or failed to recognize and address intermediate barrier conditions, then this is a failure of the process. However, if the conditions changed during the time of the project in such significant ways that it was impossible to predict or project such variations, the project success may have been overwhelmed despite excellent planning. In some circumstances unforeseen consequences of modifications could not have been identified in advance, and the resulting additional concerns may require a serious modification of the original plan. In other cases political support may be removed during a project, and in this case the resources may not be available to complete the initial project. These incomplete project results can still be seen as good, although possibly expensive, learning experiences.

While it is important to accomplish a goal, it is equally important to utilize any completion as a way to raise awareness of progress. Quite often an organization fails to promote the completion of a project. Celebrating success and/or progress is a good way to remind people that your organization is flexible and agile, and always striving to address user satisfaction within present budget constraints. Seeming to be open to many opinions and options, willing to experiment, and unafraid to make mistakes – since they can be corrected – creates a powerful message, assuming there are not too many costly mistakes. Celebrating being a learning organization that is committed to becoming or remaining a high performing organization is a good thing for inside staff to experience and for outsiders to observe.

Remaining observant and innovative, and incorporating continuous process review and improvement efforts under difficult conditions, demonstrates good management and leadership skills. The ability to complete multiple simultaneous initiatives is also a sign of a mature and well developed manager.

Ongoing assessment: meeting the original outcomes

But of course, your management job is never done, and certainly not if you have recently implemented a new workflow, service, or modification. In these circumstances it is imperative that the organization track the intended productivity against original benchmark targets, identify and evaluate any added-value that results from the change, obtain stakeholder testimonials to document the satisfaction with the revised operations, and continue to compare your operation to environmental scans for newer modifications.

In addition to providing enhanced services and creating a more flexible and agile organization, this type of post-project assessment will develop a culture that regularly explores best practices, utilizes industry benchmarks as part of normal organizational reviews and revisions, and is better able to understand, explain, and incorporate the unusual local conditions and priorities that are an important part of your operations and must be taken into account when developing appropriate outcomes.

By-product: better organizational communication and understanding

One key advantage of good project management efforts is increased cross-unit collaboration. This can be seen when the staff can better identify organizational priorities, appropriately assign project responsibilities, review and identify internal resources, proactively identify internal and external barriers to success, create and follow timelines, and effectively communicate progress and solicit user feedback during the process and after initial roll-out. Cross-library commitment when understanding the complete operation, the intentions, the decision process, and the compromises required creates a vested and more involved and dedicated staff. Resulting teamwork is far more powerful during regular operations, but even more evident during times of stress. Teamwork and morale is also improved through celebrating successful initiatives. Mature organizations also publicly learn from problems, providing a risk-free environment with documentation of best practices and lessons learned. These types of initiatives naturally lead to better cross-unit communication and future planning.

Local or contracted expertise?

When considering the appropriateness of specific project management tools, a library should consider the level of complexity required in terms of data manipulation, as with each enhanced capability there is an associated learning curve. The determination of an appropriate level of internal capability raises the question of whether a library desires to develop in-house expertise to accomplish such ongoing evaluation tasks, or whether they choose to outsource these more complex analyses to outside experts.

Maintaining in-house expertise allows a library to perform quick overviews of possible opportunities before committing any resources to more significant exploration and analysis efforts. In-house expertise also allows the library to continuously stress the importance of constant vigilance, and provides opportunities for regular training at the basic level for new or promoted staff. Proactive in-house project management trained staff will also improve communications and organizational vision, assisting with and eventually developing many types of evaluation and data manipulation skills across library operations.

In the final analysis, keep the suite of tools and available methodologies only as complex and robust as necessary. Provide the level of support required to both accomplish particular projects and also support any on-going evaluation tasks. Consider realistic timelines, realistic budget possibilities, actual staff that can be dedicated or migrated to address specific projects, and the near-future needs for serious organization-wide evaluation efforts.

Service Quality Improvement

A particular management technique that has proven very effective for identifying transformative change opportunities is Service Quality Improvement (SQI).

Service Quality Improvement is fundamentally different than re-engineering or reactive project-based modifications to identified problematic operations. SQI is an on-going philosophy of intentional management awareness, a process for continuous service review and enhancement. It involves understanding organizational missions/priorities/goals/resources, motivational issues, reviewing the effectiveness of existing operations, exploring alternatives and new possibilities based upon regular environmental scans of existing best practices, and incorporating continuous feedback and revision suggestions as part of all staff members' responsibilities. The ultimate goal is to develop and maintain a high-performing organization through vigilant attention to possibilities for enhancement.

SQI management goes beyond project management by including an overarching perspective that requires constant attention focused on improving all current operations – whether there are signs of problems or not. SQI rests the responsibility for discovering enhancements on the shoulders of all staff members, maximizing the ability of any person involved in any operation to reconsider the current processes when changes are deemed possible or recommended from outside influences.

The eyes of many well trained, informed, communicating, and vested staff members can often identify enhancement opportunities not seen by upper management with little exposure to day-to-day details about the many workflows occurring and interacting across an organization. Little reconsiderations at almost any level within the organization can lead to larger reviews and significant modifications as interrelated operations are modified, in the process discovering economies of scale and resulting in improved user services.

Over time, an organization that develops strong SQI tendencies will learn how to utilize cross-organizational teams to intuitively re-evaluate organizational intentions, effectively map and review operations and services, identify and determine best practices, and modify existing routines for efficiencies and effectiveness. It will become second nature to programmatically question all related operations when even small modifications are proposed. Not every idea that is introduced will lead to transformational change, but possible opportunities will regularly be considered before any decisions are made. Organizations trained in SQI processes will become more open to both small and large scale changes that will provide more efficient and effective services.

The key elements of SQI include the following.

Setting the stage

SQI does not happen naturally in large organizations. The tendencies in most organizations are to plan hierarchically and as isolated functional units. Staff require training and experience to break down these artificial walls between units and operate within a library-wide vision. Long-standing proprietary us-versus-them behaviors must be dropped and trust must replace information-as-power as the main driver. This alternative attitude is foreign to most organizations, and those who have risen in traditional environments must accept this new mode in which they forfeit some control in order to find new staff-driven enhancements and efficiencies. Staff used to having their ideas ignored or not implemented must learn to speak openly and honestly, with no fear of repercussions.

Many levels of training will be required to develop internal SQI expertise. There are certification programs available to develop the set of skills required to lead an organization into this new culture. It is not enough to have a few trained SQI leaders, it is necessary to have all staff understand, experience, believe, and buy into this process as powerful and beneficial – rather than frightening and not really within their job expectations. The first barriers to adopting such a holistic management perspective are based upon fears.

The managers fear that decisions will be made by well-intentioned but inexperienced staff with little understanding of the larger programmatic needs and actual competing resource claims. Many managers believe that long-term decision-making is only understood over time from developing supervision, budgeting, and service review perspectives plus an informed library-wide and user-oriented perspective. In reality, good managers have been delegating and educating staff all along and should have little difficulty expressing operations in terms of user needs and the balancing of available resources. Those managers that control information and power often fail to develop and maximize staff under traditional management methods. It may take time to develop staff skills, and you may lose staff as they themselves then move up within the organization, but this learning organization approach ultimately produces better trained and more innovative and efficient operations.

The staff in many situations have fears developed over years of experiencing crisis management and opportunistic management decisions. The staff fear the loss of jobs due to organizational redesign based upon reduced costs, fear of extra/additional work being added to existing staff, fear of inadequate training that sets them up to fail, and fear of inadequate improved performance measures due to poor administrative understanding of what is actually required and what is important within the organization at the day-to-day performance level. In addition, they have little belief in being heard and having their opinions respected by the same people that were in place in the past. They assume there will be little real change in participatory decision-making without first experiencing a serious culture change. This is why it is essential to have staff participate in the SQI training and to take on significant responsibilities in the first initiatives.

It is hard for all levels of employees to become comfortable with this new way of working across units and across hierarchies, but successful experiences will make the benefits clear and the culture will change. The organization must be willing to spend the resources and commit to the release time required from all levels of employees in order to be seen as serious advocates for this new direction. Only with obvious and total leadership support will this new approach be trusted, explored, and adopted by all levels of employees.

Identifying opportunities

SQI is a very powerful method of enhancing operations because it is always looking for opportunities for enhancements to operations. It is effective at finding significant and frequent improvements precisely because it is not a periodic or problem-driven process that addresses targeted concerns. At its most basic level, SQI efforts perform on-going reviews of all internal operations with evaluations of whether an operation is reaching established industry benchmarking standards – *while recognizing special local conditions and considerations.*

A warning should be sounded if performance drops unexpectedly over time. In addition, a serious review should be considered if a unit does not experience improvements found in similar outside operations over time due to new tools and techniques. Benchmark comparisons are excellent and inexpensive ways to identify areas ripe for workflow reconsiderations.

A standard SQI evaluation method that quickly identifies areas for targeted review is comparing existing internal workflows against best practice workflows identified through regularly scheduled outside environmental scans. It is not enough to be satisfied with doing the right thing – it is important to do the thing right. New tools, techniques, technologies, and outsourcing possibilities can produce very rapid improvements in operations that are only adopted when an organization is aware of the potential advantages. Make a regular practice of looking for ways to tweak even your smoothly running operations.

A third powerful way that the SQI process assists organizations in reviewing the efficiencies and effectiveness of their current operations is to continuously ask staff for suggestions of possible improvements to current operations. This may mean spending additional time listening to small questions, and even repeated questions over time, but it ultimately brings new possibilities to light and raises the understanding of all involved about related operational links and beneficial ways to communicate and explore modifications in a more informed way. On occasion this wide open approach to considering alternatives may introduce some extraordinary and beneficial proposals.

The more aware every staff member is of their role in the organization, how their efforts impact user services, and how the operations of other units affect their operations, the more likely you are to have creative and important suggestions. That is why it is important to train staff not only in SQI methods, but also to have them experience library-wide orientation sessions and interact with other units in brainstorming sessions. Experience has shown that significant proposals are often based upon cross-trained and cross-oriented staff members with broader cross-unit and user-oriented service views. The SQI program can provide a means of communication and exploration for new ideas, but the ideas themselves must be generated by a culture of user-oriented and exploratory staff deliberations and activities.

Performing serious analysis

Of course, SQI efforts require that all the usual project management methods are utilized. Standard project management tools and techniques that are used to track progress toward SQI enhancements include a careful and appropriate consideration of all underlying concerns, a realistic review of all available resources and barriers to success, incorporate feedback throughout the process, and are ultimately based upon meaningful and measurable outcomes.

While SQI relies upon a staff that is comfortable with participatory exploration and cooperation, and the identification of areas that are logical targets for review, no improvements will actually occur without solid analysis and creative modifications. To develop an organization that is capable of taking advantage of these opportunities, it is important to train staff in a number of analysis methods so that they have a suite of tools that are appropriate for the type of action required under any specific situation. Problem identification, brainstorming, delegation of responsibilities, data gathering, statistical analysis, creative communication with all stakeholders, flexibility under changing conditions, and maintaining focus and attending to timetables are key elements toward success. SQI training can provide some guidance and a basic set of commonly utilized analysis and decision-making tools and techniques, but an organization will need to continuously identify additional methods, and actively develop staff with expertise in the specific tools and techniques that are relevant for their own special circumstances. Developing an SQI environment and ethos provides a proven mechanism for continuously and effectively reviewing an operation for opportunities, but only creative and serious assessment will result in the desired enhancements and modifications.

Innovation potential

Another internal resource often overlooked or infrequently inventoried is an organization's infrastructure that allows it to innovate. This resource suite includes capable people with continuous support for staff training and development, assessment and evaluation, and planning and visioning capabilities. Without adequate resources dedicated to these areas on an on-going basis, you may have all the other required materials listed above and a great desire to improve and enhance your organization, but you will be unable to take advantage of the possibilities when they arise. A trained and empowered staff ready to proactively handle a variety of scenarios will result in a higher performing organization as a natural consequence and will be far more flexible and agile on a daily basis than an organization that undergoes occasional reviews or utilizes outside consultants when problems arise.

Poised for action: inside the organization

After careful analysis, document your identified staff resources and known limitations, plot out in advance any potential hindrances and barriers from within or outside your organization, chart any specific lethal time frames and drop dead dates, secure the required administrative support and advocacy, commit to freeing-up the time required by staff to identify best practices from outside, and project and plan for other allowances and immediate disruptions caused by the planning process itself. You are now ready to begin a serious service quality improvement effort.

Developing and promoting creative possibilities

Beyond accomplishing these required steps and completing the specific review, for an organization to grow into a high-performing organization it is equally important to develop the potential of all staff by exposing everyone to successful SQI initiatives. This documentation and education effort should explain the various stages, follow the progression and any unexpected disturbances to the designed steps, describe the range of options considered and implemented (including wild and radical changes that might not have been adopted), and outline the priorities that led to the final decisions and solutions. Focus should be on following a proven method to discover opportunities, but the organization must emphasize the creativity and risk-averse attitude that results in the best solutions. In addition to providing this overview and learning opportunity, it is essential to stress the absolute commitment of all involved as a necessary step to achieve success.

Project management steps

It is essential to identify opportunities, to analyze the situation and brainstorm effectively, and to commit to the program, but it is equally important to provide the framework necessary to accomplish the task on time and on budget. In addition to having a suite of analysis tools at your disposal, it is essential to have the project management skills required to coordinate the many tasks required to reach the final goals. Project management is described earlier in this chapter, and one must still follow the key elements which are to define the resources required, identify the actual resources available, designate responsibilities, define measurable outcomes and analysis techniques, create an expected timeline, and provide on-going progress reports and reviews to key stakeholders along the way.

As important as it is to reach the end of the project on time and on budget, it is just as important to use the successful attainment as a learning experience for the entire organization. Advanced and mature SQI efforts are built upon lessons learned from earlier efforts. It is therefore essential to demonstrate good initial planning, on-going progress reports and requests for feedback and additional resources due to unexpected situations, testing of revised processes against measurable objectives, and plans for continuing review. Within any successful SQI initiative is a well-conceived and executed project management plan. The best intentioned SQI efforts may fail if they are not well organized and monitored, especially as outside influences affect the entire organization.

Communicating the process and the results

Many organizations adopt and successfully implement parts of the SQI methodology. However, that may not mean that they maximize the potential available to a truly vested organization. Some organizations may be satisfied to utilize the portion of SQI that discovers early opportunities for enhancements, but they do not gain the full advantages obtained through adopting total staff participation in the decision-making aspects of ensuing reviews. Other organizations may adopt all elements of the process, but they do not push participation out across the entire organization.

To maximize the effectiveness of the process it is important to demonstrate the improvements made through organization-wide collaborations, and to especially highlight those *only* made possible through total involvement. Not only are the immediate results more frequent, more significant, and more transformative, but the entire organization becomes more effective as the satisfaction of all staff members is enhanced through deeper involvement and understanding. This will in turn result in improved operations that will result in greater user satisfaction and will generate powerful user testimonials.

The impact of assimilating the entire SQI program throughout an organization will be obvious to those within the library and to outside stakeholders. Evidence will be demonstrated through a combination of persuasive charting and documentation of the processes and the resulting enhancements, improved morale within the organization, a demonstrated increase in creativity and proactive explorations, the development of a more powerful and responsible staff, and a healthy team attitude that publicly celebrates both big and small successes.

While all of the above steps are important for a successful outcome, let us now focus in greater detail on a few of the key success variables.

Reviewing your actual resources (staff, facilities, operations, materials)

Many organizations cannot accurately describe their internal resources in terms of adequacy to perform expected tasks. This is often true of all aspects of an organization, including staffing, facilities, equipment, software, training, and planning and visioning capabilities.

Staffing

In terms of personnel, it is not always easy to monitor the adequacy of staff resources based upon reaching target industry benchmarks due to internal complexities. Each person often provides support for a number of operations, and the broad range and division of responsibilities are not always able to be tracked and compared to stand-alone task benchmarks and expectations. In many instances the multi-tasking nature of positions makes benchmarking difficult if not impossible to accomplish. Over time a number of priorities may be emphasized and revised, in some cases on a periodic and predictable basis, but in other cases based upon backlogs and outside pressures. With so many vying priorities, it is not surprising to find some elements of crisis management operating. These fluctuations in apparent productivity make analysis of adequate staffing patterns difficult, and even more complicated when tasks cross departments and delays in one unit affect the productivity and timeliness of work in associated units.

In addition to understanding and evaluating the complexities within such interdependent operations, there are other complications to be considered in terms of evaluating staff allocations. Rarely will an organization take time away from production activities in order to review minor changes in staff responsibilities across the entire operation, or even modify many job descriptions in a timely manner, as incremental changes occur within operations. It is not uncommon to have unrealistic distributions of tasks, as few responsibilities are removed from staff members when new tasks are added. As a result, unstated delay and postponement decisions occur at all levels by necessity rather than through planning and serious analysis of competing objectives. Pressure builds on dedicated staff asked to constantly work harder and smarter under unrealistic conditions. Many staff do not feel comfortable admitting that they cannot accomplish assigned tasks, and unrecorded backlogs and shortcuts may exist – and are not factored into future adequate staffing discussions.

Added to this unstable scenario are the pressures created by inevitable short-term staff illnesses and re-assignments, and equipment or outside service failures or delays. Even the best intentioned and designed short-term solutions will have unintended implications throughout the organization, and often the communication of these modifications to staffing is not transmitted immediately and widely for library-wide planning purposes. In addition, many of these short-term modifications become regularized operations, which means less sophisticated analyses are performed before new approaches and workflows are adopted. This type of quick-fix redesign is one frequent instance in which more complete organization-wide and best practices analyses would often prove far more beneficial in re-designing operations.

As much as we would like to believe that every staff resignation or retirement leads to thoughtful and well-conceived operational reviews, we know that under time and budget pressure situations many managers utilize the same patch-work approach that they develop for addressing short-term coverage issues. For many managers, it is natural to utilize these learned coping behaviors, and therefore long-term planning situations are treated more like short-term opportunistic situations. In this way the organization fails to recognize or neglects an opportunity to make significant changes after appropriate review of the broader range of possibilities.

The fact that a workflow review is possible and timely due to a personnel change may not even reach the key decision-makers. This opportunity for reconsideration may be hidden, especially if short-term drops in efficiency during times of analysis and redesign may be mistaken by higher level managers as poor unit performance rather than seen as a sign of addressing inadequate staffing to reach expected measurable objectives.

Another complicating factor is that there will always be new tasks added to operations as outside influences and ever-escalating user expectations demand new activities and services. Responsive organizations will need to implement these new services and it is unlikely that additional resources will be available for absorbing these new tasks. Never mind the lack of new staff, there will be additional pressures in just learning the new skills and absorbing the new technologies involved in the new service – while continuing to support traditional activities. In most cases, there will be little outside demand for reducing existing services, so it is almost guaranteed that additional pressure will be placed upon existing staff resources – unless the library responds by self-regulating its services based upon realistic analyses of its resources.

Once all of these considerations have been recognized, studied, and evaluated an organization will have a better initial understanding of its staffing resources. This understanding is essential in predicting an organization's ability to address future short-term coverages, longer-term planned or opportunistic considerations, and to undertake any service reviews and potential new or revised operations. In order to prepare for success, it is important to know where you begin, so be realistic in terms of estimating available staff time, and recognize and communicate any possible delays and dropped operations that might be required during intentional or unplanned periods of disruption.

Facilities and operations

In order to be prepared to maximize your opportunities, the same evaluation and documentation of existing conditions and reasonable expectations must be in place for all other facets of an organization's conditions and resources.

Organization-wide studies should be performed upon existing facilities, equipment, and software. While it is always prudent to have a good grasp of the immediate needs and present satisfaction of staff and users with existing localized conditions, as pressure builds it is even more important to be able to see the entire operation as a single entity with one clear mission. There is more flexibility and agility within a larger domain, so reviewing and planning at the organizational level provides greater possibilities for creative utilization of spaces, shared technologies, and multitasking resources.

A good understanding of facilities requirements relies on a clear understanding of program objectives and an informed stakeholder opinion about desired program support spaces. In terms of spaces, as staff and user behaviors change there may be entirely new conditions required in terms of individual quiet areas, technology clusters, group study areas, shared presentation spaces, media support, electronic and wireless Ethernet capabilities, and other underlying program needs. Traditional library spaces were developed under different conditions, and infrastructures were built with specific services in mind. There may be a need for modifications to load-bearing floors, open areas and dedicated isolated spaces, electrical and Ethernet connections, and even aesthetic considerations. Some retroactive modifications can be made to revise traditional learning spaces into more flexible active learning spaces that more fully utilize new display technologies. Other than special areas designated for rare books, quiet study, presentation practice, and supervised reading rooms, many library spaces are now less dedicated to specific tasks, with mixed use becoming common and desirable by newer generations of users.

After reviewing a number of the newer and more successful library spaces, it is obvious that what earlier library plans once considered chaotic and disruptive behaviors now occur side-by-side with few apparent user concerns. Groups of researchers use traditional blackboards beside other groups playing on gaming stations, researchers mash media technologies beside individuals working on collaboration workstations. In some cases rooms are divided by decibel levels rather than activities, and many users prefer to study in the loudest areas, even if they are working in isolation. Flexibility with spaces and furniture and user-determined alterations to configurations are highly desirable. Control of spaces is now seen as detrimental to the development of the best learning environments that increasingly emphasize group behavior and technology-sharing needs. Given the many conflicting desires for facilities, and the new dynamic and novel combinations of spaces and tools, a complete re-purposing of the entire library facility provides far greater opportunities for creative solutions.

The accompanying increase in electronic books, maps, databases, and journal materials may also allow for a reduction in the requirement for physical staff production space and shelving ranges. New media, data, and GIS support labs may become a new priority if other buildings do not provide such areas and central services.

The new trend toward blended or fusion buildings provides spaces for very different activities, far beyond the now common interactive Information Commons spaces, and may include sports and recreation areas. Most libraries now allow for, and in many cases include, some form of food and beverage services. A new balance must be found between traditional service support and new teaching, research, and recreational elements. These new blended approaches challenge many assumptions from the past, but evidence shows far greater utilization of all embedded services.

A grasp of desired space needs, possible space renovations, the competing priorities for space, conflicting space requirements, and resources for space modifications is necessary in order to begin discussions of short-, medium-, and long-term building evaluations.

In libraries of all types, equipment support requirements are constantly changing and organizations should regularly consider re-alignments of staff technologies. With the migration of many tasks and online support activities pushed to distributed individual workstations, there may be less need for central and dedicated staff technologies such as separate staff printers and copiers in all units. On the other hand, it may be that some units find it cost effective to migrate from individual printers to shared printers, regardless of whether they are dedicated to staff only. Similarly, many machines can now perform all the formerly individual tasks such as copying, scanning, printing, and fax. A blend of appropriate equipment for the specific levels and intensities of the tasks is now possible, making customized and more efficient and effective technology support possible. A thorough review of support technologies may result in savings, more current services, and improved support for all users. It will certainly position a library to better adapt to new practices and procedures.

It requires no great observational skills to recognize the fact that user technologies are undergoing rapid and unpredictable changes. Mobile technologies, proprietary software, wireless interconnectivity, and new multi-purpose equipment are now appearing daily, and users expect the latest technologies to appear immediately. For instance, while libraries continue to support traditional photocopying (and often rely on revenue from copy services), most libraries now need to upgrade and offer free scanning and internet delivery options. In the past our concerns were with coordinating our photocopy and printing operations using a single charging mechanism that addressed both internal users and visitors. Now we must also address questions of validation before offering distribution mechanisms that can carry significant security and legal implications. Given this proliferation of free and networked capabilities, many libraries have chosen to remove cash operations, change machines, and petty cash services. This reduction in cash handling satisfies auditors and eases some staff safety concerns, but it can create problems for visitors without local permissions or credit cards for handling any service charges.

Software and even hardware support is now possible using remote servers, saving costs for dedicated expertise, 24 hour clean rooms and redundant servers, and other support considerations. In some cases it may be far less expensive to share the cost of a cloud-based server among multiple institutions. The trade-off for shared support can often be a lack of customization and a time lag in making modifications and corrections. Remember to consider the hidden costs of support if your software requires local servers rather than cloud-based support; this can include maintenance and upgrade fees, add-on module costs for local customization, additional storage space costs, and regular staff training and travel expenses.

Open source software may now provide equivalent service, and great savings can be found in some areas when migrating away from expensive and often underutilized commercial software to inexpensive, if not free, open source software. Our local IT (information technology) officer always reminds us that free software is like a free puppy, not like free beer – there are follow-up maintenance costs involved. Consider these hidden costs when making a fair assessment of potential savings from a migration to a collaborative and possibly less stable, but more flexible, system.

Maintaining current and compatible software across operations can provide better efficiencies and open new avenues for collaboration, analysis, and documentation of operations. While it will always be necessary to have some special software for specific tasks, it is best to utilize standards-based tools to provide organizational integration. Most operations can only support a limited number of operating systems on various platforms. Be programmatic in selecting which technologies to support, and what level of support you will provide for any particular tool.

Libraries often feel pressured to provide at least a minimal level of support for competing user tools. For instance, in terms of handling statistical and GIS (Geospatial Information Systems) data, libraries often provide software for Stata, SAS, SPSS, and ESRI products. Libraries may offer a limited number of seats, or they may work with other campus units to provide site licenses for the entire organization. This is where economies of scale may be important, especially if you can go beyond contacting the traditional teaching units and involve operational units such as facilities and community outreach. Some libraries also provide additional software that targets particular communities such as Simply Map which is marketed as a business tool, but which can be used by researchers in many other disciplines.

Knowing when and where to cut off software support is a difficult challenge when users expect libraries to be on the cutting edge of data support. And we have not even discussed the associated costs for providing orientation and instruction, or even more time-intensive consulting support for these software products. A library must decide where it fits into the organization's coordinated support model, and allocate appropriate resources to meet the ever growing expectations for manipulating and re-purposing information and data for users and decision-makers.

Offering proactive and integrated information-handling skills for administrative purposes provides an opportunity to demonstrate to decision-makers the added value that a library can provide when it delivers service beyond simple data discovery and storage. Examples of valued services include comparative studies of organizational publications and production to peer and aspirational institutions, assessment of the impact of instruction and librarian involvement on the quality of final products, return on investment studies of grants received to production, and providing data for staff recruitment and retention or tenure decisions. There is no better way to develop advocates from important stakeholders, and while you may already have the software, this additional service does have associated staff costs that must be absorbed. In the long run it is a wise investment of time and effort that will result in greater support.

In the following case, one considers the advantages of organizing budgets along functional lines. Such structured budgeting does not inhibit library-wide planning and communication, but actually allows for better planning for cross-unit operations. Alignment of budgets by function allows for tracking specific resource allocations and performing detailed assessments of efficiency and effectiveness. It also allows for consistent service evaluations over time.

Case Study 7: Creating a budget aligned to functions rather than personnel

As a new Director, you arrive and ask the service coordinators to provide a review of costs per service. You immediately discover that there are no detailed budgets in relation to operational tasks. It is almost impossible to discover how much resource is dedicated to a particular operation, be it staffing, equipment, or other expenses. This is a direct consequence of the organization having a "flat" organizational structure and hierarchy, in which the organizational chart has been developed based upon people rather than functions. There is no way to follow particular tasks in terms of time, resources and effort.

Any plans to perform effectiveness and efficiency assessments compared to industry standards are immediately much more complicated. To begin any type of quantitative analysis, you start by asking each service director to approximate costs per service, based upon designated staff time and invoice estimates. After these estimates are compiled, you compare these numbers to industry standards to look for large anomalies that might identify areas which might be improved after review and modification. You also begin to work with the budget officer to develop a task overlay on top of the existing budget, which will allow you to perform more accurate assessments in the next year. Finally, you ask the library staff to consider the costs and benefits associated with various alternative organizational structures at a future meeting.

Now let us look at the implications of various organizational structures in terms of service reviews. Many organizations have very hierarchical structures which closely mimic the functions they perform. This functional structure makes budgeting and review easy, as there is a direct correlation between resources and tasks or services. However, this functional aspect of the organization can reduce creative and proactive conversations across and among units, especially when there are multiple processes that ultimately serve the same user population. At the other extreme, an organization can function quite well without such strict functional hierarchies if communication and planning are well coordinated. In such flat or alternative organizational structure scenarios, the tracking of costs is performed using a shadow system which records resources dedicated to each task as if they were individual projects. This mirror accounting system can become complicated and burdensome in large and complex organizations. The corresponding benefits of such alternative structures and infrastructures can include a more open culture and might also produce a variety of by-products such as novel cross-unit functional relationship representations across an organization. The costs include maintenance of parallel service tracking systems and a need for more vigorous training to maintain an involved and empowered staff. In summary, while it is possible to create a second system that monitors resources for each element performed by individuals in order to track task-specific expenses, it is often far more effective (especially in large or complex organizations) to create an organizational structure based upon tasks in order to have this resource information easily aligned with and accountable to priority services.

In this particular organization there was no shadow tracking system developed for recording resources by function. Creativity may have been developed under this looser model, but there was no easy way to demonstrate the effectiveness of the resulting operations against industry standards. Given the lack of either hierarchical or functional reporting data, while it was possible to follow expenses by person, this reporting of task-based resources became problematic when one person was responsible for supporting more than one service or function. Under these circumstances it was impossible to assign specific allocations to particular tasks. This lack of tracking by task meant that it was not possible to clearly evaluate the cost and therefore the return on investment of the tasks under review. The same difficulty existed for assigning and assessing equipment and financial resources to specific tasks within multi-function units. This lack of detailed non-personnel resource tracking made analyses less specific and meaningful as well.

User satisfaction could be measured, but it was not possible to compare the underlying costs to best practices in similar organizations. Effectiveness and efficiency measures could not be correlated in a meaningful way. Ideally, you would like to have data that shows creative involvement and also demonstrates excellence and efficiencies. In difficult financial times it is required that you support claims of creativity and agility with quantitative proof of efficient impact as well as testimonials from satisfied users.

Why were flat structures so popular? It was the trend at one time to create flat organizations in order to improve communication and involve all staff in decision-making. Decisions were often made at the top of an organization, and problems arose due to a lack of knowledge of the day-to-day operations and/or unintended impacts of proposed modifications. It was felt that traditional hierarchies that utilized task forces to cross unit lines and encourage cross-unit collaborations were not flexible and agile enough to allow for maximum staff involvement and creativity.

In many cases an administration resisted dedicating resources to improve internal cooperation and flexibility. This hesitancy was often based upon mistakenly perceived resource requirements. When considering the time and effort involved, administrators failed to differentiate between the reasonable resources required to establish helpful cross-unit orientations as opposed to the enormous and intensive resources required to develop cross-unit training with the intention to incorporate shared and overlapping duties. The communication and creativity improvements in hierarchical organizations would be gained from understanding related tasks and impacts, not necessarily from being able to perform all related tasks. Even when full cross-training was provided, less productivity and greater tension were often observed as the infrequently transferred staff demonstrated (and were aware of) a reduction in competencies due to irregular job experience. Any advantages gained from greater appreciation of related tasks was often more than nullified by losses in productivity and the introduction of more frequent errors. In some instances of well-designed cross-training, advantages were seen in terms of coverage in emergency situations and a better understanding of the impacts of library-wide services. But all too often, over time, cross-unit communication and cooperation was not supported at the level desired to encourage and support significant participatory decision-making.

The implementation of efforts such as Total Quality Management (TQM) did increase all staff involvement in decision-making and resulted in more flexible and agile organizations. However, what were sometimes lost in many such TQM-like approaches were two things. First, there was a loss of detail about the individual functional support operations. The newly merged operations were not always supported with task-based resource allocation tracking documentation. In these cases, the improvements in effectiveness of operations due to better cooperation initially masked and marginalized the resulting inability to evaluate the efficiencies of the blended operations. As budgets became tighter it was no longer good enough to be better than previously, it was now necessary to demonstrate that the operation was as efficient as possible. This is when it was realized that tracking each operation in terms of cost was needed if the modified reporting lines and budgets no longer provided such detail.

Second, there was often a failure to assign ultimate authority for a project to an individual, a key part of the original Japanese model, and many projects failed to reach completion as difficult decisions by groups were unable to reach a consensus solution and progress stalled. This authority concern was addressed by assigning authority and regular progress reporting responsibilities to specific people or subgroups within the larger communication and planning team.

As pressures increased and assessments and modifications were expected, it became more obvious that without task tracking regular progress reports could not include specific costs and detailed assessments. The solutions were to either create shadow tracking mechanisms or to revert back to task-based organizational hierarchies and provide better cross-unit planning and decision-making groups for creativity and agility. Both solutions can work, and you will still see both structures in place in many organizations. Fortunately, many organizations that have moved to flat structures operated without serious budget problems and were never forced to address the tracking concerns. When financial pressures started to exert their influence, and decisions about efficiencies and effectiveness were paramount, these organizations quickly became aware of the need for task-based tracking.

Other management concerns that arise from an organization that utilizes a flat organizational chart include:

1. it is difficult to show cross-unit and cross-task relationships when there is no clear locus of control for specific tasks,

2. it is difficult to monitor historical trends and modifications to services (in relation to changing influences), if there is no permanent resource record for each task, and

3. it is not easy to chart aspirational plans and demonstrated accomplishments and savings to specific services and tasks.

These types of historical relationships and histories are much easier to observe if the organizational structure is obviously aligned with library services and priorities.

It is always more difficult to make priority decisions with less than adequate or desirable amounts of information, and it is equally difficult to delay these important decisions while you gather the required data using newly implemented procedures. Just think of how difficult and time-intensive it is to make these priority decisions even if you have the information, and even more so if you first need to learn how to analyze and prioritize the options. The lesson is: be as prepared as possible with all the data and analysis tools at your disposal before a crisis arrives. Have the task-specific costs ready for when a review is required or desired.

For resource tracking reasons alone, it is often easier and more effective to develop a primary organizational structure around tasks and operations rather than creating two systems, one aligned with the people and the second designed for resource allocation tracking by task. In addition, creating a structure and budget aligned to functions rather than personnel allows you to maintain long-term and consistent records of task-based allocations, as opposed to a shifting set of supporting resource streams as individual job responsibilities change over time, as they often do.

Outside factors and influences

Feedback from informed stakeholders

Opinions are important, but informed opinions drive organizations toward success. Too often an organization limits its potential by not envisioning and presenting the best possible service model to those making allocation and priority decisions. It is almost impossible to advocate for new services if you are unaware of their existence or potentials. Stakeholders must be pushing for better services based upon knowledge of exemplar libraries.

Surveys and support

How often are surveys sent out to users asking which services they most appreciate? First, users only appreciate those services they have utilized. Immediately your analysis and their input are limited to the level of activities they have experienced, rather than the full suite of potential options you already offer. In addition, surveys are self-selecting, so you will often only hear from the outliers – those very pleased or very dissatisfied. While this is the easiest group to contact, this is not a representative group on which you should base your future service profiles.

Even when a library utilizes gap analysis techniques, gathering correlated data on the importance of a service and satisfaction with the present services, this more sophisticated analysis is still limited to ranking your present operational offerings. LibQUAL+ and other tools can provide useful information on where your users feel you should concentrate your efforts and resources, but they only consider existing services. You need to describe other possibilities and measure their importance.

Well-designed surveys start with descriptions and demonstrations of all potential service options. Only when users can understand what is possible, beyond what is known or currently offered, will they provide informed opinions on what are the broadest set of highest priorities. While describing new services may seem helpful, it rarely makes an impact on busy researchers and readers. Experience has provided one important lesson in terms of introducing new possibilities: show – don't tell. Self-referential demonstrations are proven as the best way to show users how new services can save them time and provide new and helpful tools with obviously powerful results. This type of preparation will result in both better informed survey opinions and stronger advocacy for a well-designed organization. There is no stronger supporter than one who has seen and experienced the power of a new service and is willing to assist you with passion in your striving toward achieving that result.

Becoming the portal of choice for access to unique material

Another issue in gathering user feedback is that many library users are unaware of which resources are actually provided to them by the library, or that the library provides different types of information that may be important when they are looking for credentialed material. Libraries must start by making users understand that the library should be the portal of choice for certain types of information gathering, and that the library is their only means of access to enormous numbers of resources that are not provided by free information tools. Better branding is required to emphasize the library's importance and essential role in providing access to their desired information. More intuitive and attractive interfaces and some level of online or face-to-face training are probably required to have readers begin their investigations at our online spaces in order to obtain access to all the available for-fee information we provide. If users will not start at our web sites, at least they should be aware of the need to be routed through our resolvers in order to gain their allowable access. Only an informed and aware user population will gain maximum benefit from our resources and then be able to provide the type of input and support that propels libraries on to greater services.

Addressing user expectations

Conversely, there is nothing harder to address or manage than explaining why an organization fails to meet user expectations, even if those expectations are unreasonable compared to existing resources, legalities, or community needs. Once a powerful service has been experienced users will desire that level of support, and a library must seek to provide something close to that service if at all possible. Even a partial service or a referral to other organizational partners or outside vendors is better than simply stating that the service is outside the scope or range of the library at the present time. Appearing to understand and communicate the benefit of such a desired service is the first step in dealing with disgruntled stakeholders. Asking them to imagine how your organization might move toward that service for their particular population involves them in problem-solving and integrates them into your future decision-making group. Even if you are never able to satisfy the request, you may succeed in having them gain a better understanding of your priorities and competing interests. This may form a deeper bond and develop a mutually respectful relationship that may provide other types of support. Support is what you strive for when you are a service organization, especially when many of your products are not obviously provided by you but are seen as free on the internet, and when other providers (e.g. Google, Yahoo, City Map) seem to provide easier interfaces.

In the following case, one witnesses the power of utilizing informed user feedback rather than relying on anecdotal perceptions. The appropriate prioritization of services requires an understanding of user and stakeholder needs and desires. With this important information in hand, a library is prepared to reconsider the services currently offered and present new possibilities that resonate with important user populations.

Case Study 8: Understanding and meeting user expectations: internal reports

A library staff member announces their resignation, and after a thorough review of the operation by the administration, your boss announces that the person will not be replaced. Each person will need to work smarter to accomplish more, and the unit will re-evaluate services and perhaps alter the level of service or even drop certain historical services in order to address the gap between resources and reasonable expectations.

A review of current library services and budgets identifies a target reduction in service support hours. Each member of the team is assigned a set of tasks to review and is expected to provide alternative support models per task ranging from "essential and impossible to reduce efforts" through "drop the service entirely".

One of your areas for review is: News Reports which are provided to the upper administration. These reports are executive summaries and annotated news links in specific subject areas which are compiled weekly by the library staff after exhaustive searching of online news resources. These time-intensive internal reports include summaries of new developments in various research areas of importance to the corporation, they include current research updates from the corporation in related areas, evaluations of current corporate initiatives compared to these research programs, and projections of impact in the short and medium term on corporate activities. Based upon anecdotal evidence, basically positive comments from a few executives, it is believed that these reports are at least important, if not still essential.

A survey is performed across the organization to determine the key elements within these reports that are considered top priorities. Surprisingly, most administrators were either unaware of the reports or were unimpressed and stated that they did not review them. They preferred to use existing industry RSS feeds to remain aware of general news and to identify key competition factors. They stated that they valued the credentialed updates from their industry colleagues, made their own interpretations of these news factors, and did not utilize the summaries and internal analyses provided by the library staff.

The few administrators who were known to have scanned the reports, and who had casually mentioned that they were interesting in the past, were then contacted for clarification of the discrepancy between the survey results and their earlier comments. They admitted that they did not consider the internal reports important – they were merely providing positive reinforcement to staff about a professional looking effort in their earlier comments. Many stated that they were unaware of some of the other industry RSS feeds until they were contacted by the staff during the follow-up, and they were now going to utilize those important tools. The one person who did look at the internal reports as casual reading that might raise some new ideas also stated that he would now be satisfied to review the existing industry RSS feeds instead of the internal reports.

Based upon this information it was decided to stop the News Reports research, development and distribution efforts. This released a good deal of time from two research staff members and significant production work from another Outreach Department staff member. This time could then be re-allocated toward other priority tasks. Similar analyses uncovered other efforts that could be scaled down or eliminated, and it was possible to absorb all the important tasks from the previous employee with existing resources.

The biggest problem identified as a result of this review process was not one of reducing important services, but instead was political – how to explain why the loss of an entire position could result in the loss of so few meaningful tasks, especially when the corporation had been asking for leaner operations for quite some time. It would be clear that a thorough evaluation of the services offered by the library was long overdue. While reviews and subsequent re-engineering efforts had been performed by library staff to create more efficient operations, it was now obvious that an important missing element of a well-designed service evaluation had been the review of existing services by the key stakeholders.

In order to avoid potentially embarrassing displays of negligent management action, which arise more often during difficult financial times, it is best to be proactive about maximizing resources. This starts with understanding your changing users' needs and desires. It is dangerous to believe that historical and anecdotal feedback represents current conditions. It is important to first educate your users about new tools and techniques that are available by demonstrating what is possible after performing thorough environmental scans. Once your user base understands what is possible and has spoken for and witnessed implementations of their most important preferences, maintain contact with these important stakeholders by performing regular surveys of satisfaction and by presenting any additional new options. This continuous service quality assessment process will uncover areas for purposeful abandonment of less important historical services, and identify new and changing opportunities to react to revised and relevant priorities. In this way you can generate savings, enhance and improve existing services, and demonstrate your sensitivity to changing conditions.

Assessments: some initial and obvious first analysis opportunities

Examples of assessment opportunities exist throughout an organization, but first attempts can be focused on small projects with obvious and immediate benefits. These areas for successful demonstrations can be identified by looking within your organization for services in which you already collect data that can be analyzed and then compared to industry benchmarks. Some areas in which many libraries collect data (even if they do not actually fully utilize the resulting information for organizational redesign) include the use of reference statistics software to track levels and types of activities (for future staffing and service coverage modifications), data gathering for instruction and one-on-one consultation sessions (for reassigning subjects to librarians based upon actual effort), and compiling typical cost/effort charts and effort per population data for collections and subject librarian time analyses. All of this data must be considered only elements to be handled as weighted variables, and nuanced evaluation is required as not all efforts are equivalent or of equal value.

Service Quality Improvement efforts require a serious organizational commitment. Regular and in some cases intensive training, the recognition of the necessity for staff release time, dedicated financial resources to support such on-going activities, educational awareness efforts targeting user populations, and consistent advocacy for the need for reflection when pressures exist for maximum productivity, are just some of the elements required to maintain awareness and proactive efforts toward continuous process and product improvement. These commitments are not easily made, nor are they easily maintained, but they are essential for maintaining a very flexible and agile organization. Leadership support determines success, but complete staff participation creates the greatest potential for success.

Reference

Zhang, Y., & Bishop, C. (2005). "Project-management tools for libraries: A planning and implementation model using Microsoft Project 2000." *Information Technology and Libraries*, 24(3): 147–152.

4

Understanding and utilizing data and statistical reports

Abstract: Good managers make decisions after gathering only as much information as necessary. Gathering data and knowledge from within the organization and benchmark data from outside is important, as is incorporating a full suite of data analysis tools and techniques. Managers should utilize a blend of qualitative and quantitative analysis techniques, and should understand the inherent characteristics and limitations of various data gathering and presentation techniques. With an understanding of the goals and the available resources and expectations that surround the task, it is possible to study the relative effectiveness and efficiency of various options. In addition to measuring productivity or effectiveness, it is important to measure user satisfaction and perceived values of services. Quantitative measures of efficiencies demonstrate good resource management, but do not underestimate the persuasiveness of well-utilized qualitative data.

Key words: data, qualitative, quantitative, analysis, surveys, reports.

Collection and analysis of appropriate data

Good managers make decisions after gathering as much information as necessary to understand the many variables and possibilities that are in play. Gathering data and knowledge from within the organization and from outside is important in reviewing all considerations, reasonable expectations, and options. Incorporating a full suite of data analysis tools and techniques makes a manager more able to respond to a wide variety of situations with appropriate measures. The better you understand the variables involved, the more you are able to develop sophisticated and innovative solutions.

Qualitative measures

The best managers utilize a blend of qualitative and quantitative analysis techniques. Some services are only measurable in qualitative ways. When qualitative measures are combined with knowledge developed through years of experience and perception, and evaluated with an understanding of the goals and the available resources and expectations that surround the task, it is possible to study the relative effectiveness and efficiency of various qualitative options. You may not be able to measure the exact productivity or effectiveness of all services, but you can measure the satisfaction and value of the operations in comparison to more quantifiable services.

In the end, remember that as a service organization, you are hoping to develop what are recognized as responsive and satisfactory services for your users rather than just the most efficient services. Quantitative measures of efficiencies will impress those with little understanding of your services, and the ability to appear to be a good resource manager is certainly important when competing for resources. However, demonstrations of quality service through satisfaction measures and strong advocacy by users will never fail to impress those with influence and decision-making power over your resources. Do not underestimate the political power of well-utilized qualitative data.

Quantitative measures

In other situations the service under review easily lends itself to quantitative measurement. Or at least a portion of the tasks can be measured and assessed compared to industry benchmarks. Such measurement is important if you want to both maximize the effectiveness of the operation and demonstrate your effectiveness to those allocating resources. While measurable data cannot always demonstrate the value of an operation, it can often be used to show the satisfaction and the effectiveness of services.

The important data

In order to most effectively gather and utilize data in decision-making situations, you must understand the nature and limitations of the data you require. You must also recognize the lack of value of some data that may have been gathered over many years; data that may have been easy to capture but which serves no purpose other than for statistical reporting. One thing to purposefully abandon is the collection of meaningless data and statistics.

Let us now look at some of the important considerations when working with data. We will also consider the appropriate application of this information toward resource allocation requests through the use of powerful and persuasive statistical reporting.

Evidence-based collection and analysis of appropriate data

The first rule of collecting data is only gather statistics that matter. While most activities can be measured in some way, and some measures of efficiency or effectiveness can be captured, in general remember that you are only interested in those statistics that might make a difference for measuring success or for evaluating modifiable efforts. Unless you need to capture data for reporting purposes beyond your control, stop gathering any data that cannot be utilized for evaluations leading to meaningful organizational modifications. Your data will be more accurate and reliable if you only gather what is important, and if your staff understand why and how the data will be used. There is negative value in collecting and maintaining useless data.

Data characteristics and limitations

Quantitative analysis begins with data – good data, appropriate data, understandable and useful data. While a discussion of data analysis is beyond the scope of this book, there are a few basic considerations that must be mentioned.

Understand the accuracy and validity of your data. Do not make the classic mistake of performing deep statistical analyses on generalized or representative data that does not contain significant enough detail or elements to offer accurate estimates or deduced knowledge. For instance, do not utilize a few weeks of random reference desk statistics in order to analyze and determine appropriate hourly staffing patterns. There is simply not enough data and refinement for such a determination to be made. At best you may use this rough data to provide limited support for an intuitive or commonly held belief about conditions in similar libraries. Be careful not to overestimate the value of your data, especially when dealing with small sample sizes.

Try to handle value-laden data in such a way as to differentiate opinions about the importance of a service from opinions about the performance of such services. Be careful not to let opinions and feelings unduly influence categorizations or rankings of services. Using gap analysis techniques allows users to provide separate measures of their opinions about the importance of a service versus the quality of the service. LibQUAL+ and other tools rely on this gap to identify areas that require the most immediate attention.

Understand the conditions under which your data was captured. Data taken during exceptionally busy or quiet times will skew overall results unless you factor in these variables. Data gathered during unusual circumstances will not reflect normal behaviors, and you should note such conditions if you are forced to use such data. Especially if you intend to track data over various time periods, attempt to gather data during similar conditions. Remember that there will always be some new conditions and variables, and record these influencing factors in order to consider them during analysis. For example, adding and circulating new digital tools (e.g. cameras, laptops, tablets, microphones, calculators, etc.) will significantly increase your circulation counts. Changing loan periods will influence your renewal counts. Migrating to electronic reserve material will modify your circulation figures and some behind-the-scenes staff efforts will no longer be reflected in your numbers. Be prepared to describe the changes in the data and discuss new ways to capture the efforts and the service measures.

Survey data

Survey data may include a number of problematic issues. Below are listed a few common concerns that must be considered.

Beware of relying upon skewed sample responses. Often the results obtained in surveys are, by nature of the gathering mechanism, only providing responses from self-selected segments of your population. For instance, an online survey will only reach those researchers who are comfortable enough online to trust and spend time answering a series of questions to a machine. Whether we like to admit it or not, many people avoid or ignore their email, which is where the survey link will be found, and they will not participate. Others will never enter any demographic information into a survey, and they will stop before even reaching the first question. Still others simply refuse to interact online, but would complete a paper survey. Even with online surveys that appear automatically during or after information interactions, many people refuse to spend their time answering such questions, considering them invasive or bothersome. In these cases, the responses you receive are often from the minority that is either very satisfied or very dissatisfied.

How often do we start a survey only to leave after a few responses because the questions are so badly written that the meaning is unclear or too simplistic to answer given the type of responses allowed? Creating quality surveys that capture accurate quantitative information about the intentions of the participants requires skill and planning.

Creating surveys with the correct type of response continuum to reflect the type of questions and possible range of responses requires an understanding of appropriate methods. A poorly designed survey will provide data that can be dangerous if analyzed using inappropriate techniques.

Trends and indications may be generated and reported when the underlying data does not really support such conclusions, based upon concerns such as poor handling of multiple variables or inadequate breakdowns of responses to show significant differences in responses. Consult an expert before you create a survey if you intend to perform any deep analyses of ranges of responses.

Quite often people create quantitative surveys to try and capture qualitative feelings. This can be done using special techniques if you understand how to display the range of feelings correctly and how to accurately measure these responses. The analyses that are appropriate for handling qualitative responses are also different than those used to represent quantifiable data.

Staff-gathered statistics

Obtaining adequate, appropriate and significant feedback from surveys can be difficult. Quite often the response rate is so low that the data should not be handled as valid representational input. One would think that obtaining accurate and realistic data from paid staff would be much easier: in some cases the software captures data as transactions occur, in other cases interfaces are designed to make statistical capture fairly simple and relatively non-invasive. However, when the workplace is hectic people often forget or skip the recording of data in order to provide better immediate service. It is not uncommon for manually entered data to disagree with associated software captured data; for instance the IM/chat software records far more interactions than are documented on the manual record of transactions. Often this may be due to quick box closures by patrons before a response is given, hardware failures, and other technical situations such as users jumping to another window and losing the original chat box. But a portion of the differences is caused by staff not entering the transaction data due to overwhelming activity, forgetfulness, or intentional disobedience. The disobedience can be caused by a number of factors including a desire to not have your efforts tracked and reviewed, a refusal to perform administrative requests, a failure to care about the statistics because you do not understand the importance of data gathering and analysis for improving services, and the ultimate counter-intuitive barrier – data burnout. Quite often the sheer amount of tracking that occurs creates lethargy and resistance – either intentional or unintentional. Statistics are in some ways like signage – too much of it means you ignore it all, and staff may actually detest the attempt.

Data purposes may drive entry and accuracy

The solution to these obstacles is to keep statistics gathering to a bare minimum. Only capture what you need and can utilize. Only capture data when you need it; if you only need representative samples do not constantly capture the data. Explain to staff and users why you are gathering data, the purposes and impacts of the data, and the implications if inaccurate data is captured. A vested audience often provides more reliable data. However, in some cases unobtrusive data gathering is preferred in order to find normal behaviors, as it is not unheard of that data is manipulated by knowledgeable persons to produce special interest results.

Compare to exemplar results

In addition to gathering local data through a variety of methods, in-house data should be compared to benchmark data gathered from outside parties. It is important to base your analyses on industry standards obtained through environmental scans of other organizations. Professional associations can often point you toward best practices and benchmarking standards. Some of this information is held in private consulting firms which will charge you for an institutional review, but a significant amount of comparative data is recorded in the literature in journal articles, technical reports, or association reports such as the ARL SPEC Kits. Assessment and service enhancement success should not be measured merely by some improvement; you want to become as effective as you can be compared to other well-designed operations. Do not just be better than you were, be the best you can be.

Using data effectively

Having the data is just the start of any effective analysis. To be successful you must know how to perform accurate, meaningful, and persuasive presentations. This requires an understanding of organizational priorities, immediately available resources, stakeholder desires, and eventual benefits. You may have all the data required to demonstrate an enhancement that either saves money or improves services, but if it is not presented at the right time or presented to the right group of decision-makers it may not be supported. Timing and presentation will almost always trump facts when making decisions about reallocating resources if personal interests and competing factors are involved. Of course you must focus on having the right facts to support your position, but you want to develop a strong argument that involves stories that touch emotional trigger points.

Perform effective evaluations

Familiarity with data, and the ability to at least minimally critically evaluate quantitative and qualitative data is a key skill for any staff member, as every employee will be asked to review some level of performance, be it their own or a group that includes them. Treat any required evaluation efforts as an opportunity for training staff in assessment techniques, reinforcing group responsibility, and as an opportunity for mentoring less experienced staff in management and leadership skills that will help them advance and help the organization perform more effectively.

The right data

In order to perform an effective and meaningful evaluation you must understand your intentions, your available relevant data, your immediate possibilities and the range and scope of these variables, and your realistic expectations and organizational convictions. With those conditions understood, select the most appropriate evaluation methods to provide useful supporting information. Your success measures should be measurable and comparable to expectations and results from other similar organizations. It makes no sense to provide very deep statistical data about complex solutions that you have no realistic possibility of adopting. Your analysis should only be as deep as necessary.

The meaningful data

Focus on key measurable elements, those with the highest values for success and failure. Do not let what amount to small (although sometimes threatening and personal) concerns delay or distract an organization from moving on accomplishment of big successes. Demonstrating large impacts is far more important than pointing out any small and measurable savings or losses that might occur due to the modifications. Be sure to mention necessary tracking of related and influenced activities throughout the organization, and plan to measure and assess the incidental impacts and positive by-product enhancements that your modifications might produce. Remember to consider and highlight any short-term peripheral support that might be required during the transition and evaluation stages. Provide a fair and balanced overview of impacts across the entire organization.

The right tools

Utilize appropriate methods and tools. There are many types of statistical analysis, and each is designed for handling specific types of situations with particular sets of elements, variables, and conditions. Outlining the variety of tools and techniques is beyond the scope of this book, but you can find some excellent overviews in standard statistical textbooks. Also consult the "Suggested readings" at the end of this book. If you are unsure of the validity of these techniques for your scenario consult a trained statistician who can provide the advice and insight you require to select the best tool for your analysis project.

Adjusting the weighting of variables

One rule of thumb to remember is that when dealing with many factors (such as costs, various population sizes, classes of populations such as students and faculty, use data, and grant funding), it is often advantageous to use a regression analysis that allows you to weight the variables to determine how relative priorities will affect final distributions. Of course this flexibility means that it is possible to tweak the initial weightings in such a way as to obtain support for a desired outcome. For this reason using regression analyses without clearly determined and agreed upon weightings can be seen as dangerous if some members of the team have predetermined priorities.

As always, remember that statistics can be manipulated and presented in ways that prove many different perspectives. Treat statistics and analyses carefully, and be sure you are cognizant of the bias that you include through your treatment and presentation.

Utilizing statistics

Once you have gathered the appropriate data, selected the appropriate tools, weighted your variables according to your organizations priorities, and performed your evaluations you will have processed data that can assist an organization in recognizing logical modifications to priorities, operations, and enhancements.

Current operations in relation to standards

The results of statistical analysis can provide an organization with both specific details of current operations and visualizations of trends in operations over time. Studying current measures will aid in the identification of areas for attention when local figures do not compare favorably to industry standards and expectations. Many organizations concentrate on improving the immediate efficiency of these easily determined areas of under-performance. Improvements are easily seen and measured after implementing best practices. Statistics are used to discover and document process improvement and service quality improvement.

Indicators to recognize

Where many organizations fail to take advantage of statistical possibilities is in recognizing and acting upon more subtle trend analyses. These performance patterns can be studied as indicators of organizational agility and responsiveness, offering overviews of productivity, efficiency, and effectiveness. Careful review of these measures can highlight potential opportunities – areas requiring, or positioned for, significantly enhanced results after targeted attention and modifications. These patterns can also be studied and manipulated in order to create projections of resource expenditures and future problem areas. Sophisticated managers scan for trends and propose proactive solutions to potential problem circumstances. They excel by transforming details into indicators and by acting as problem solvers and crisis avoiders rather than crisis managers.

Building persuasive statistical arguments

The first thing to remember when making a presentation is that a library carries inherent cachet and goodwill. Knowing that you are already seen as a valuable and important organizational entity, keep your presentation positive. Talk about satisfaction measures and enhanced services, and do not introduce negativity, as this will deflate initial good feelings and result in a loss of group energy. Demonstrate the quantitative concerns and treat statistical measures as facts rather than endowing data with negative values and emotions. Regardless of the present conditions, the conclusion of the presentation should remain optimistic, enthusiastic, and invigorating; showing any troubling trends in the context of possible solutions and desired services. A persuasive presentation will inspire people to advocate because their hopes and passions can be aligned with a specific goal and they believe they can make a difference in facing the challenges.

Know your audience and select your key points and demonstrable enhancement opportunities based upon the desires of these key decision-makers. Find personal areas of interest to make relevant points that resonate. While you may have efficiencies that seem important to you, and they may align with established organizational priorities, they may not always excite and activate your stakeholders. If you excite your listeners with powerful examples they will entrust you with the resources required to accomplish their desires, and these will also address your internal concerns.

Utilize simple and powerful graphics. Images can demonstrate distinctions and patterns far more easily than rows and columns of data. Visualizations tap into visceral understandings far more quickly and powerfully than verbal descriptions of data. The intuitive element that is touched by graphics fosters deeper associations than the complex interpretations garnered by exploring logical mathematical considerations. These impulsive feelings generate support from both the head and the heart, which is much deeper.

Remove any data elements that do not immediately and powerfully support your key points. Distraction is bad for many reasons beyond simply losing the focus and the story you are attempting to convey. Including irrelevant information in a presentation shows an inability to focus and target on key issues, a failure to understand and be sensitive to audience concerns, a lack of awareness of time management, and questionable critical thinking skills. While framing and storytelling are important aspects of persuasion, presenting only the significant and relevant content is essential to carry a persuasive position.

Display your data in a larger context in order to give the values meaning that the audience can understand. Data does not carry relative meaning until it is compared to something else with documented values. Show present services and evaluation data in relation to existing benchmarks, trends, and aspirational organization measures. Compare your conditions to those of peer institutions to address a sense of pride as well as powerful and significant evidence for any resource requests. Then show your present and target figures in relation to exemplar organizations to generate a competitive spirit and a commitment to excellence.

Assuming you may not immediately convince all stakeholders that your entire request amount is essential, be prepared to provide multiple models of services, with implications for service quality along the various phases of implementation based upon the allocation level. Start by describing minimal targets and services, but conclude your summary by demonstrating the full suite of services possible with the maximum allocation. Regardless of the level of services you describe, be sure to demonstrate each target service in terms of personal impacts for individuals by including the following: convenience, added-value, and novel options. Appealing to personal desires and describing relevant researcher benefits is always more understandable and persuasive than highlighting impersonal organizational savings or enhancements.

Remember that all this quantitative evidence exists to support an emotional argument for additional resources. Your goal is to create qualitative beliefs and supporting testimonials that demonstrate your effectiveness as a planner and a manager. You may have occasions to directly convince the decision-makers if they are in your audience, but often you will be attempting to persuade your primary clientele, and their enthusiastic qualitative testimonial support powerfully supplements any quantitative evaluations when presented to upper-level administrators.

In the end you are creating a story, and the data helps to set the stage, to build the support required to carry you through the challenge, by effectively appealing to organizational pride, and by fostering and directing the enthusiasm and empathy of the audience toward mutually agreed upon and measurable objectives. Measurements should be emphasized to demonstrate success and to generate pride.

In the following case, a variety of important data analysis concerns are raised and considered as a library develops a process to impress and assure users that they appropriately included both qualitative and quantitative evidence when making a difficult political decision. Complexities of underlying emotions and behaviors, and of the data itself, are honestly expressed in order to obtain buy-in with the process. Local considerations are emphasized, and fairness based upon return on investment analyses is presented as deciding factors. In addition to involving users from the start in order to build trust, the entire process can be utilized as a learning opportunity for all involved.

Case Study 9: Evidence-based decision making: journal profile modification

Administrators of all units within an organization are informed that due to the poor performance of the company's stock portfolio, there will be across-the-board cuts in the coming year. Based upon additional considerations, selected units may receive some relief while others will be cut more deeply. In follow-up private conversations, library administrators are told to plan for no additional relief or further cuts beyond the standard reduction. Now the library administrators must plan for the coming allocation reductions. For this case, we will focus on one of the most flexible and significant portions of the library budget, the journal subscriptions, which account for approximately 40% of library expenses. In this organization there are no internal charge-backs within the company for library services, so there are no revenues generated by the library that might be redirected. In the future the library administration may look into creating virtual charge-backs for services in order to supplement their current understanding of where the resources are most utilized, and therefore identify where these resources are most valued, and perhaps where additional support might be available for maintaining specialized tools.

It is understood from previous experience that any reduction in journal subscriptions will have negative effects across the entire organization both in terms of delaying access to actual research support and in generating strong emotional reactions. Knowing this is the case, it is essential that the review process must include evidence-based decision-making, but it must also address other political concerns.

Even within the more objective evidence-based analysis, there are different types of data. The first essential type of data to be gathered and analyzed involves journal title usage. This usage data is supplied by both the online vendors and through in-house reshelving counts of paper titles. The use data itself has inconsistencies; some of this use data may be refined to the detail of publication year, but not all title-use data includes the year of publication for accessed material. This level of detail is important for performing accurate assessments of the value of current year versus backfiles and embargoed data sets. Some access is measured at the actual fulltext article retrieval level, while other platforms can only provide access numbers for hits on the bibliographic landing page which provides Table-of-Contents level access. In the latter instance it is possible that some readers may have stopped at the extended abstract and not continued and obtained value from accessing the actual fulltext. The manually counted paper use data may be undercounts as it fails to account for items reshelved by users, even though there are signs asking for the material not to be returned to the shelves. In addition, we know that many people access fulltext articles from author sites, institutional repositories, subject pre-print servers, and other free or aggregated sources. These numbers will not be reflected in the standard COUNTER-compliant numbers provided by the original publisher or by the data coming from shared journal platform hit counts. It may be possible to obtain use data from some of these outside providers, but many do not report this access information at the institutional level. These are just a few of the complications that must be recognized when working with the best hard data in the analysis. The accuracy of the analysis becomes even more fuzzy as the data itself becomes even more subjective.

In addition to the actual use data, there is another important measurable element that should be captured – the perceived importance of specific journals by each member of the user population. This type of qualitative information is subjective, but the overall results can be compared to the somewhat more objective Journal Citation Report rankings to identify special local considerations that must be accounted for in the weighting of factors during the final analyses. It is not uncommon to find that this perception data may provide information that contradicts the actual use data. We are now looking at a situation in which the most measurable factual and impressionistic data clearly contain ambiguity and approximations.

Any additional estimates of relative values across journals must take into consideration many other variables that might be related to the previously mentioned use and perceived use data. One type of use-related calculated data that is important to include in an analysis involves the merging of associated cost data. It is necessary to consider cost-per-title, cost-per-article, and cost-per-use figures. These derived figures can be evaluated for effectiveness when compared to alternative purchasing and document delivery options. Unfortunately, there are uncertainties within the cost data as well. First, the cost of journals is not always exactly the same as the listed catalog prices due to factors such as service charges and package discounts. Package plans can make reasonable title costs almost impossible to determine as there is no accurate way to calculate the true value of the add-on titles that come with a Big Deal package. Even the value of the most expensive titles changes over time as add-on title use becomes a more important element within the package value which might erode the initial stand-alone value of the original high-use and high-cost titles over time. Another concern is that these cost and value figures can be easily misinterpreted when comparing titles across disciplines which can exhibit very different behaviors, involve varying population sizes, and display very different publication characteristics.

Another type of variable for consideration and weighting is the nature of the journal use; for instance, is the material utilized for research support, is it primarily a teaching tool, is it important as a trade journal for insider industry news, or is it used for providing high-level overviews and for scanning for trends? Perhaps it serves to provide a general awareness of the political climate, is used as occasional recreational reading, or it provides non-standard technical reports and grey literature from industry consultants. These are important information distribution facets and each has its own relative values within the research literature lifecycle. The important characteristics must be recognized, documented, and appropriately reflected within the analyses.

There are even new types of tools still being charged to traditional journal budgets that are actually online newsletters and virtual communities that offer important networking services such as shared best practices, directories, software and equipment reviews, and job boards. Should this review exercise serve as the impetus to create new types of budget lines to handle the special characteristics of such novel resources, or is it better to wait until after the journal review to make such alterations to supporting infrastructures? If the modifications are deemed quite complicated and require serious review before any action is taken, remember to put this concern into the parking lot for later attention so as not to lose track of the required review during the excitement of downsizing.

Do not forget to recognize and weigh other general and discipline-specific characteristics when assigning value to journals. Example considerations to identify might include factors such as the importance of journals versus other formats in a field, the typical citation half-lives for a discipline which will affect the importance of backfile and embargo concerns, the presence of cross-discipline, undergraduate and core curriculum support materials versus pure research materials, and the relevance of political imperatives such as supporting local editorial board members and local editorial offices, providing favored society support, favored SPARC and Open Access support, and other local stakeholder considerations.

Remember that this assessment task should also be considered an opportunity to focus attention on these important issues as part of an ongoing educational and current awareness program. The best supporters, especially during difficult financial circumstances, are those users and stakeholders who are aware of how well you understand and can describe the many competing factors involved in identifying the most appropriate resources. The stakeholders can also utilize this knowledge to their own advantage when they are in a position to influence larger organizational politics by effective lobbying, as they know best how to interpret and present these data analyses for maximum impact.

The actual analysis begins with looking for obvious signs of misalignment between resources and impacts. Before you even look at the use data, review the general allocation figures compared to the populations and any characteristics these disciplines might have that would create large discrepancies. For instance, it is important to know that business and science journals are far more expensive than social science and humanities journals in general, and this will explain the much higher allocations in these areas. It might also be important to recognize that certain fields do not highly value journal publications compared to other types of distribution mechanisms, and their allocations will intentionally be skewed away from a fair percentage. The first reviews are focused upon the fairly simple to calculate cost-per-population ratios. At this initial stage identify unexpected anomalies that require further examination.

Once you have been able to explain or identify any unusual population-related allocations, it is time to see if the Return on Investment (ROI) appears to be equally beneficial. To study the alignment of allocations to impact, start by reviewing your figures that were calculated based upon the raw use data. The most important impact calculation is cost-per-use by population. It is important to look for gross anomalies in these figures, but remember that local conditions can create startling differences in these impact numbers. It is always good to cross-check very strange numbers against other sophisticated ways to determine impact by population – such as by comparing your local numbers to the Impact Factors calculated for general populations by the Web of Science. Your initial investigations and considerations of possible reductions and re-allocations should be based upon a balance of demonstrated impact and other factors that relate to local priorities.

These first two steps help an organization to quickly identify obvious outliers based upon a review of the relevant raw numbers. Now it is time to add the more delicate and complicated factors to the decision-making process. This next phase of the assessment becomes a matter of finesse with variables rather than just brute force with evidence.

Some of the complications to consider when selecting potential journal reduction titles are:

The initial use data seems to provide some measures of value and impact, but it is important to recognize that the sheer variation in the size of the researcher populations makes the potential for swamping effects a very dangerous element. One title can have far more impact in a smaller population of researchers or a smaller number of title subscriptions than the impact of most titles in a larger population. A ten percent cut can be far more devastating within a small number of titles than within a larger number of titles. Preferential cuts may be necessary to lessen the relative impact of cuts across very different size initial sets of subscriptions.

Not all titles are equal from the start, as survey data will determine that some subscriptions are perceived as untouchable, and should not even be considered as possible cancellation targets until another phase of reviews is necessary. This untouchable designation may be disappearing for very expensive and little-used titles due to the introduction of new seamless document delivery options.

A major factor in reviewing potential reduction targets is the impact of journal packages or Big Deals. These packages often involve multi-year contracts with associated inflation and cancelation caps, making large numbers of titles and large portions of the journal budget unavailable for reconsideration. The advantages of these package plans are that they allow for predictable budgets, provide access to larger numbers of titles than previously owned by any one library, and reduce the year-to-year inflation rates. The disadvantages include a loss of flexibility of the largest portion of the journal expenditures budget and difficulties in determining the actual value of specific titles within the plans. As stated earlier, it is misleading to use the list prices to determine the cost-per-use and ROI values for these aggregated materials. In some cases it is impossible to obtain access to some titles without a package plan, and new titles are often introduced as part of a plan with no opt-out option. New seamless document delivery mechanisms that cross publishers are making the value of the Big Deal less appealing to some organizations that do not see as much benefit from access to the less frequently used titles in the package. A new and more flexible budget may be developed utilizing a balance of subscriptions to key titles and somewhat less predictable costs for immediate and seamless pay-per-view options. The removal of a lag time or intermediary support for non-subscribed titles provides a new way to obtain materials that frees up resources compared to the restrictions found in many package plans. Many titles previously treated as untouchable due to purchase method rather than content may now be reintroduced to the review process. The maturity of package plan purchasing and more sophisticated data analysis and delivery mechanisms may allow us to move toward more effective use-based options. During tough fiscal times effective delivery of required journal materials is far more important than simply offering more titles that are infrequently used for the same price. Difficult fiscal situations may move us more quickly toward a just-in-time approach rather than continuing to support a somewhat obsolete just-in-case publication model.

Another element to consider is how to best address the historical uses of journal materials. Subscription plans often include only the current year, or in some cases the past few years of published material. However, many uses are for older materials that are not covered in the current subscription deal. In many cases the use data does not provide the granularity to even determine what percentage of use is for current versus backfile material. This is important if one is to calculate accurate impact and cost-per-use data. The correct analysis of this historical use data may allow libraries to reduce redundant or overlapping subscriptions if the purchase or lease of backfiles is not a priority, or in the opposite direction if the use of an aggregator with an embargo period would still be a satisfactory alternative to a current subscription. This is where combining actual local use data with citation half-life characteristics may provide some creative and less harmful journal title reductions during tough fiscal times.

The composition and implementation of the survey document itself can strongly influence the effectiveness of the analysis. Some organizations are satisfied to have a single response to journal priorities by a department, while others require input from each researcher. The most effective type of survey obtains the granularity required for considering both qualitative and quantitative data in one pass. Each researcher should associate their particular demographic characteristics (which will be anonymous in later reporting) with the value of each title under consideration. Is a title essential for research, important for teaching, infrequently used for various purposes, or not important? This information can be converted into quantitative values, and when merged with the actual use data, it can provide quick clusters of high and low priority titles. Essential research and important teaching titles are removed from consideration immediately. Not important titles can be placed in the first consideration pile, for later comparison to any package plan limitations. Infrequently used titles can be ranked using the actual counts of votes, and priorities can be determined for relative importance across disciplines by accounting for the initial sizes of the voting populations. If each researcher provides this information at survey time the important calculations can be made quickly based upon real data, as opposed to requiring a later painful second survey process if only one response per department is obtained. A second review of the titles will already be required before any actual reductions are made, so why add yet another round of surveys?

The survey document should provide a brief description of the situation and the intended process in order to ease suspicions and demonstrate that there will be ample opportunities for interested researchers to be participants in the entire evaluation process. Make the initial survey instrument as granular as necessary to complete a thorough analysis. Some surveys contain use and cost data for each title. Use and impact evaluation data should not be placed on these initial surveys, such distractions should not be important factors in obtaining what you seek at this point in the process – researcher impressions of the utility of the materials. This type of calculated information should only be distributed at the stage of making actual cancelations along with the total counts of votes by demographic breakdown. Keep the evaluation separate from the opinions, and involve everyone in the larger considerations once all the qualitative and quantitative data has been compiled and presented for consideration.

Once the data has been compiled it can be presented as important elements required for a thoughtful group decision. The data should only be used as one set of indicators, providing a degree of local information about perceptions, use, and impacts in relation to expenses. The data presentations may provide direction for early considerations, but they will not determine the ultimate decisions, as these conversations and negotiations will involve many other political factors. It is not appropriate to use this new data to try and change earlier decisions about the impacts of reductions; that discussion has already happened. Make the data presentations informative, but not prescriptive. The data can suggest certain actions, and these should be proposed as logical possibilities, but do not appear to be completely data driven in your considerations. Let the stakeholders recognize the negative impacts of these conditions, and allow them to lead any motions for reconsideration of resource allocations to a higher authority. Have the data available to support such a political movement, but do not lead the conversation as it will be far more persuasive coming from the user population.

The presentation of the data and supporting analysis should also address additional considerations that may strongly influence ultimate decisions, whether their positions align with the data or not. There are a number of important political implications to consider when contextualizing the compiled data to interested stakeholders. For instance, how do you address any unique revenue streams? Do you choose to mention that certain researcher populations may already differentially support the library resources through indirect cost sharing such as grant overheads, departmental subsidies, and contributions of selected personal journal titles? In terms of special interests, do you push to support short-term expenses for the sake of potential long-term benefits by supporting Open Access titles that might provide alternative solutions but are now based more upon altruistic desires than realistic business models? Do you support institutional Open Access memberships that reduce author fees even if your organization will not see any actual savings or might even pay more? Will you remove some titles from consideration because your organization has members on editorial boards? Will you protect your organization from accrediting reviews by supporting titles with high impact factors even if they see low local use? Finally, are there political reasons why you can or cannot designate priority disciplines, or must you make across the board cuts or only modify targets using apolitical factors such as cost-per-use-per-population?

In the end there will be a document explaining the entire process, the underlying values and judgments, the ranked list of titles to be reduced, the alternative delivery approaches to be used, and the expected impacts which will be monitored by a specified process and reported back for future reconsideration. The review should be seen as well designed, minimally disruptive, and completely transparent. The decisions may have been painful, but the process should be seen as having been handled professionally under the unavoidable and difficult financial circumstances.

In this journal reduction exercise it is possible to see the value of gathering the right types of data, the power gained from utilizing the most appropriate evaluation methods to demonstrate impact and ROI, the importance of considering and delicately presenting the additional political factors and other implications that might influence the decision-makers, and the advantages to be obtained by involving all stakeholders in the assessment in order to have them understand the scenario and obtain maximum buy-in with the ultimate decisions.

This process was far more than a data gathering and analysis exercise. It was a complex interaction with users and administrators that resulted in greater understating, respect, and perhaps even new and enhanced services.

Internal reports

Present the initial and revised findings and continually work toward improvements

The results of an analysis should be reported to both internal units and key external stakeholders, while the messages and supporting data provided should be tailored to the interests and knowledge levels of the individual groups. Brand them from your group and make them clear and precise; treat them as executive summaries with pointers to supplementary information.

Use internal data presentations as a way to celebrate improved or adequate results and build pride as you compare your organization to outside entities. The best way to present a difficult analysis report back to internal units is to provide constructive criticism rather than failure documentation. It is well documented that a small amount of constructive suggestion is best delivered with a large amount of positive feedback. Providing opportunities for immediate feedback, and not defensive explanations, is an important way to gain understanding, buy-in, and shared next actions to enhance existing operations and results. This is how you develop a learning organization that enjoys exploration rather than fears attention.

Remember to roll-out any reviews within the larger and long-term vision of the library. Show how the specific initiative aligns with the organization's Mission and with overall priorities, unit goals, and individual SMART goals. Create your report points to coincide with the key elements of the organization's strategic initiatives. Make it obvious that there are immediate benefits to organizational leaders, all levels of staff and your users. Emphasize the long-term benefits in terms of quality, efficiency, productivity, prestige, and brand recognition, and show everyone you have the backing of strong advocates and all are committed to seeing inspirational results.

Continue providing reports

Statistics and their associated analyses should not disappear when you have obtained your desired resources. You should provide updates to internal and external stakeholders as service modifications are made, and as summaries of actual measures are compared to target measures and changing outside standards over time to demonstrate continued success and effectiveness. People who commit to a service improvement process expect feedback, they are partners and should be treated as participants throughout the initiative.

They should also be kept aware of related service improvements or new potential initiatives. Communication wins you support if you have the right data, and communication wins you continued support if you demonstrate success and sensitivity to user needs and desires.

Suggested readings, tools, and contacts

While it is beyond the scope of this book to provide a comprehensive or even representative sample of writings about Project Management, the following short list of materials will provide a beginning list of readings, tools, and consulting bodies utilized by many libraries. There are many tools designed for specific applications, so be sure to explore other options before undertaking any large-scale actions.

Biafore, Bonnie. *Microsoft Project 2010: The Missing Manual*. Sebastopol, CA: Pogue Press, 2010. Print.

This book offers details, examples, and perspective from a skilled project manager.

Chatfield, Carl and Timothy D. Johnson. *Microsoft Project 2010 Step by Step*. Redmond, WA: Microsoft Press, 2010. Print.

For beginners, this book provides step-by-step directions on how to use the Project software. For the more experienced, it offers a quick reference guide to utilize unfamiliar options.

Horine, Greg. *Absolute Beginner's Guide to Project Management*. 2nd ed. Indianapolis, IN: QUE, 2009. Print.

Provides practical information for the beginner.

Larson, Erik. *Project Management: The Managerial Process*. 5th ed. Chicago: Irwin Professional Publications, 2010. Print.

Good depth of coverage for the serious learner, and includes many case studies.

Larson, Erik and Clifford Gray. *Project Management with MS Project 2007*. 5th ed. New York: McGraw-Hill, 2010. Print.

This good introduction also includes the Microsoft Project CD with a free trial period.

Madsen, Susanne. *The Project Management Coaching Workbook*. Tysons Corner, VA: Management Concepts Press, 2012. Print.

A detailed workbook to guide leaders and team members through the many stages of a successful project management process.

Tools

Microsoft Office Project 2010 (*http://www.microsoft.com/project/*). A popular commercial product that offers sophisticated project management capabilities, therefore provides enough lead time to address the required learning curve.

DO (*https://do.com/*) is free software that helps groups create and share tasks, projects and notes. The software also integrates with Google products. Premium options are available for a fee.

Google Sites – Project management template (*https://sites.google.com/site/pmwikiboot/*). This pre-created template includes a calendar and work spaces for other important elements of a project to be recorded, but it does not provide actual project management functionality.

Associations, training, and consulting firms

International Project Management Association (*http://www. ipma.ch*). Compiled by a non-profit organization with the aim to be the "prime promoter of project management internationally, through its membership network of national project management associations around the world".

PM World Today (*http://www.pmworldtoday.net/*). An online portal that contains articles, papers and stories, regional reviews, book reports, and project reports related to professional project management.

Project Management Institute (*http://www.pmi.org*). An American non-profit professional association which caters to certified managers, promotes professional development, facilitates the exchange of ideas, and describes the fundamentals of project management for beginners.

PM project-management.com (*http://project-management. com/*) is a portal site that provides free current awareness about recent articles and reviews of PM software programs.

LAC Consulting & Project Management (*http://www.lac-group.com/lac-consulting-project-management/*) is a company that provides library and information consulting and project management services.

4pm.com (*http://www.4pm.com/index.htm*) is a company that trains and certifies project managers.

5

Environmental scans and the power of best practices

Abstract: A key component of the Service Quality Improvement methodology is continual review of current operations against industry best practices. The creation of an organization that is flexible, agile, and responsive to user needs is most effective when all staff are involved in reviewing and improving both operations and policies. Modification explorations should consider alternatives from non-traditional industries, but all deliberations must include a careful review of local characteristics. Phasing in modifications is a delicate task that requires a balance between acting upon pressing user needs and maintaining an organization's ability to withstand pressures without experiencing debilitating trigger events. Internal scans will demonstrate successes and the power of total teamwork.

Key words: Service Quality Improvement, environmental scans, best practices, exemplar institutions, staff involvement.

Service Quality Improvement (SQI) involves a total reconsideration of organizational intentions, priorities, operations, and decision-making. The ultimate goal is to create an organization that is flexible, agile, responsive to user needs, and efficient and effective. This occurs best when all staff are aware of the ultimate services and work toward continuously reviewing and improving the means toward that end – both the operational details and the underlying policies. The culture must be one of participatory questioning of status quo conditions and searching for better methods and most appropriate services. In difficult financial times it is even more imperative to keep the focus of questions on user-oriented goals rather than on short-term savings.

While adopting new approaches may provide immediate solutions to crisis situations, a high-performing organization stops and considers the long-term impact of modifications before adopting new policies and procedures. Many modifications to practices and policies are always possible, and a thorough scan will discover a variety of considerations that work well in various environments. A careful analysis of how local conditions and expectations will be impacted is required before seriously considering implementing newly discovered tools and techniques. Selecting the right modifications is important, as any organization can only absorb a limited number of simultaneous disruptions and remain stable. Phasing in modifications is a delicate task that requires sensitivity to a healthy balance between acting upon pressing user needs and expectations and an organization's ability to withstand pressures without experiencing debilitating trigger events.

Steps toward identifying best practices

Focus on the right variables

The first step in reviewing and revising local practices is to determine your actual target concern. In Chapter 3 we discussed using techniques such as Interest Based Problem Solving to identify actual problem conditions rather than just addressing symptoms of deeper concerns. When looking at service targets be sure you have adequately analyzed and addressed the intended user service outcome and not just the present operation. Remember the difference between "doing something right" and "doing the right thing". Study the underlying intention in relation to your specific mission, vision, targeted goals, and measurable objectives. Target the expectations and priorities, not the immediate situation.

Visualize elements for clarity and impact

One method that has proved effective in helping organizations to stay focused on the big picture is flowcharting an entire organization rather than just specific processes. Visualize the larger goals and document the associated processes and operations using flow charts. This holistic approach allows you to observe the ultimate goals, the intended targets, and the paths toward reaching the desired results. Paths are adjusted to reach targets, resources are assigned to particular paths, and success is shown as increases in productivity or satisfaction toward mission-based service targets. Visualizations are effective ways to see both intentions and progress at the same time. Remember how effective maps and bar charts were when you visited the zoo and instantly were able to see the global distribution and level of endangerment of the animals? The same intuitive and visceral reaction can be obtained by visualizations that highlight and demonstrate goals, plans, resources, and progress.

We will assume that you have involved all appropriate staff and stakeholders and can now clearly state your desired service and measurable objectives. It is time to scan the horizon to seek previously existing solutions that might satisfy your concerns and needs.

Find similar studies

It is unlikely that you have an absolutely unique situation, and it is quite possible that a number of organizations have developed and demonstrated effective methods that can be modified to address your local needs. It is possible that these procedures have either been described in the literature or discussed within professional associations or workshop settings. The library literature is full of how-we-done-it-good articles, and many of these include literature reviews that highlight key articles that provide additional considerations you might benefit from reviewing before you make final decisions. Web sites from library associations and other related entities contain pointers to best practices for specific services and difficult scenarios. These tools may point you to groups or individuals familiar with similar conditions. There are also a number of library consultants who operate in various areas, offering experience in providing customized solutions for various library environments.

Compare ROI when possible to address complexities and qualitative measures

Your goal is to be effective. An effectiveness analysis includes measuring efficiency – but how do you measure efficiencies in complex and multi-process operations with competing resource needs? You start by measuring your present operations, in terms of Return on Investment for expended efforts and resources. You then compare your results to the

ROI results from other approaches through side-by-side tables of measurable data whenever possible. Not all products and qualitative satisfaction factors can be measured easily or quantitatively, so you must be prepared to compare the importance of these less definable attributes as well when comparing satisfaction results to recognized gaps in important services.

Focus

Do not look for all possibilities for every organizational function. Concentrate your scan on those operations that resonate with your local satisfaction points. Clearly delineated priorities that result in focused scanning are the keys to effective explorations. It is important to know what to target so you bring back the right observations from among the many potentially distracting processes you could study.

Satisfaction is found by addressing local concerns. Your intention is to create customized priorities and processes that address your informed stakeholder expectations. Your scan should result in the discovery and promotion of relevant aspirational services and processes.

Scan broadly

When performing a scan it is important to stay focused on the ultimate goals, but do remember to think and scan broadly. Search beyond your normal industry to discover novel and relevant procedures. Seek out large-scale solutions from other industries that might apply to your operation. Best methods and approaches are not always already implemented in your peer institutions, many important solutions may be found in related industries. For example, you may find best practices for shipping book materials within procedures used by large shipping companies that are not normally associated with libraries. In this instance, as the result of looking beyond your current scenario, you may be able to either implement new shipping methods or propose new price models that prove advantageous when dealing with vendors that have not looked outside their industry and modified their perspectives in many years. Your solutions may include the modification of outside operations. In difficult financial times all organizations are looking to modify for efficiencies and effectiveness; this might be a good time to discuss revisions to existing conditions, contracts, and processes.

Expectations

In performing scans, be sure to notice or search for underlying expectations, either stated or implied. While many organizations do not post customer contracts, it is possible to determine certain reasonable performance measures that are minimal aspirational targets. Look for things such as turn-around times for book delivery, document delivery, Rush Order processing, and Reserves processing. Look for statements of quality service, and methods of obtaining and responding to feedback. These are indicators of well-designed operations that have seriously considered user expectations within their operational plans. Ask such organizations if they reach these measures, and determine what their priorities are if they need to dedicate additional resources to accomplish these desired levels of service.

Remember that not all user expectations are reasonable, and users often misunderstand even stated expectations.

Quickly drafted and posted policies may be too simplistic, and are therefore dangerous if they unintentionally create unrealistic user expectations. Keep your stated expectations related to publicly demonstrated industry norms. For instance, many people believe that processing time for e-book orders will become inconsequential through immediate and seamless patron-driven acquisitions (PDA) processes, but this is not always true. While ebooks ordered through OPAC discovery may be immediate, requests for previously published materials may be more complicated. In one example, an attempt to quickly replace a missing paper copy of the Merck Index with an electronic copy was delayed as background considerations involved numerous parameters such as the desired host platform, the potential reference tools bundle in which it might be co-located, the number of simultaneous seats, and the format of the resulting materials. Clearly described and realistic expectations will help avoid some future frustrations. Look for organizations that demonstrate an understanding of the complexities through nuanced statements to their constituents. These may be the best places to begin exploring best practices.

Local considerations

Regardless of where you look, how hard you look, and who helps in the search, there is no such thing as *the* best practice for an operation. It is important to remember that one organization's best practice may be totally inappropriate for another organization under different circumstances. A particular SQI initiative requires you to identify the relative effectiveness of possible alternatives, and a thorough evaluation determines success measures that speak to your local needs and goals.

Who looks?

Given the many local considerations and factors involved, an organization must ask itself: Who should be involved in scanning the landscape?

A successful scan is determined by the acuity of the searchers, so the rule should be the more informed the eyes the better the results – and the greater the number of perspectives the better the odds of finding a good option. For this reason it is important to have a wide range of staff involved in scanning the landscape.

In the best possible scenario, all staff would be involved in scanning for new tools, techniques, and trends. In practical terms, it is reasonable and advantageous to include members of the staff from various levels and across related units when performing web-based or site-visit explorations. Small modifications, and associated savings or new services, may only be observed by those already performing the day-to-day tasks. Processes are composed of many small details, and only those deeply involved will be able to see the potential small and large benefits of intricate alterations to current operations. Novel impacts, unintended positive deliverables, and disruptive consequences may be initially uncovered when associated operations are considered by a range of staff members during targeted explorations.

It is not only the broadest staff perspective that is important. The perspective of endusers and stakeholders is essential if an organization is hoping to identify new and enhanced service options. Stakeholders may be able to see impacts of modified services even when such enhancements are not clearly recognized by the library itself. What may go unrecognized, or may seem a by-product to the library, might be a key deliverable for users. Only the users themselves can know the full range of what might be important to them when looking at possibilities. Involving the stakeholders in the search for new options creates a stronger level of understanding in potential advocates, and a stronger human bond. Searching is a natural human behavior, and a well-run exploration results in a positive sense of teamwork and shared experiences that will provide future benefits.

Performing Service Quality Improvement analyses

Selecting the right projects

Many new practices could be implemented, but will they result in significant enhancements to services? Change for the sake of change can be costly in terms of disruption, resource expenditures, staff morale, and delayed organizational development. Once goals are targeted, scans have been performed, and options have been identified, an organization is prepared to analyze the effect of implementing these potential best practices on obtaining desired measurable objectives toward enhanced services. Effectively identifying projects for completion is a key to maximizing resources, especially when resources are tight and every new action delays alternative efforts. Continuous awareness of opportunities does not necessarily result in constant SQI activities. Careful analysis may screen out possible projects with only small impacts compared to the effort required. SQI projects should result in significant alterations or transformational actions in order to make the effort worth the time. Not every non-action is wasted effort, as an initial SQI scan may discover areas in which less intensive re-engineering may be an effective way to address small modifications that will result in small gains in productivity.

Obtain staff commitment

Service Quality Improvement analyses require total commitment in order to see all levels of potential impact and all potential enhancements. SQI cannot be a top-down process, although it requires high level advocacy, encouragement, and participation. How does an organization create conditions that support such long-term involvement and total investment? First it must be recognized that any design for evaluating local situations, potentially modifying existing operations, proposing staff re-assignments and requiring training, and resulting in facilities changes generates natural fear and resistance. In order to calm such concerns it is necessary to regularly remind all staff of the long-term user goals, and demonstrate that the changes are both necessary and wise. In this way you will obtain support, celebrate success, recognize staff and stakeholder satisfaction, increase a feeling of security for a better trained and appropriate staffing plan, and generate strong advocates for future initiatives. The best way to demonstrate intelligent SQI actions is to strive for meaningful measurables, targeting services that clearly satisfy users, keep staff involved and committed, and emphasize not just efficiencies but rather effectiveness in relation to all stakeholder desires.

It is also important to keep the entire parent organization aware of your conscious commitment to continual enhancement efforts, and of the successes. Public updates are important to both administrators and staff. Administrators benefit from being recognized as proactive by all members of the community. Staff members develop better self-esteem and pride when their organization is seen as innovative and positive.

Observing organizational results

How does one know when success has been reached, and that it is time to celebrate? There are some obvious signs demonstrating movement along the continuum toward becoming a high-performing organization. Look for these as early indicators, and use them to motivate staff and excite your advocates.

The first sign that an organization is adopting effective SQI practices is that all staff can demonstrate they understand the importance of developing continuous effectiveness measures for their key services. The next stage is having identified service priorities, with associated operational workflows and simple measurable objectives. The third stage of SQI maturity is demonstrating that the organization is performing scans to identify the best practices for their key operations. A very mature organization can demonstrate that after analyzing and modifying their operations they are composed of more effective and efficient operations. Celebrate each stage as an important step toward becoming a learning organization. Adopting these perspectives and becoming skilled in these techniques takes time and deserves to be applauded along the way.

Another way to see results of effective SQI efforts is to observe a gradual migration toward more appropriate services. Notice the de-emphasis of historical efforts – this rarely occurs without a serious analysis of operations, even under difficult financial times. Purposeful abandonment is a conscious effort that rarely occurs without pressure, and you know you have succeeded when you see such dropped services aligned with the start-up of new and more appropriate services. Organizations that adopt new tools, techniques, and trends must make tough choices in order to free up resources from existing operations. Those that do not

147

perform serious analyses often dilute all operations – some to dangerously inadequate levels to satisfy user expectations – rather than make sound long-term resource decisions.

Another indicator of success is incorporating sophisticated user opinions in your operations. The act of measuring user satisfaction is a sign of good management. The measurement of informed opinions is a stronger sign of involved and satisfied information users. Even better is the satisfaction measured from user advisory groups, those users interested in helping to develop new and enhanced services of direct interest to particular user populations. This type of deeply invested participation leads to advocacy when and where it counts most.

Two other indicators of a strong SQI organization come directly from the organization itself. The first is that you recognize a willingness to question current operations, thereby creating a stronger learning organization and higher levels of change potential. The more each member of the staff understands their role and where modifications can improve services, the more likely they are to be comfortable suggesting alterations or areas for investigation. This is a healthy sign of a mature staff that is not afraid of their place in a transforming organization. In such situations it is not uncommon to witness the advancement of line employees into supervisors and managers based upon creativity and observation powers.

The second internal indicator of advanced SQI initiatives is the existence of good documentation for prior activities and of lessons learned. These reflective materials serve as the foundation for continuing reviews and revisions of best practices. They assist the organization in focusing on relevant and appropriate services. One important document to locate is an organization-wide updated flowchart of key goals, operations, and SQI initiatives. This indicates a long-term approach to SQI with measurable results.

With these unmistakable indicators of appropriate environmental scans and SQI implementations, the improved performance and morale of a high performing organization will be evident to internal and external stakeholders.

This type of progress and positive teamwork is even more impressive when witnessed under difficult fiscal circumstances that are inevitably and relentlessly imposed upon libraries due to outside factors. SQI initiatives make opportunistic actions look both obvious and innovative.

Remain aware

The best scenario is when an organization develops into an aspirational operation, and others visit you to see best practices in action. Even when you work in a state-of-the-art scenario, a commitment to SQI still requires constant vigilance in order to adapt to new conditions. Too often great organizations stop implementing the tools that helped them become flexible and agile through relaxing their commitment to regular self-examination. Becoming proud often results in complacency, and that is a recipe for disaster in such a dynamic and volatile industry. It is ironic that just when an involved staff becomes most powerful the self-satisfied administration reduces the potential influence of this hard-earned skill and knowledge. Few organizations succeed primarily through the efforts of only the managers, but many fail due to their negative influences. SQI remains a team effort, regardless of the present development of the staff and the effectiveness of the present services. Just like in martial arts, awareness is always required if one expects to react appropriately. In martial arts heightened awareness is expected in combat situations, and in libraries heightened

SQI activities are required in difficult financial circumstances. As is always the case, but even more so in difficult times, being better than your competition requires diligence and constant practice.

In the following case, you will observe how mission, strategic planning, supporting evidence and underlying special interests are exposed and balanced to determine the best approaches to enhancing services. Developing a common language and understanding among all relevant staff allows for a powerful scan of possibilities, and may result in far more impressive products than originally conceived. This inclusive approach also results in greater trust and better library-wide communication and problem solving.

Case Study 10: Best practices for analytics and web interfaces

Due to recently announced budget reductions, the library will need to reduce expenditure and revise its current services. As the head of Collection Development, you have been informed that you will have a new and lower allocation for databases in the next fiscal year. Your charge is to develop a new mix of subject indexes and databases that satisfies the majority of current users and reduces the present spend. You will be working with the subject librarians over the next ten months to reconsider the databases themselves, and you recognize you will need new tools to evaluate usage. In addition, you are not certain that the present web site adequately promotes the full range of tools you currently provide. You will also ask the subject librarians to reconsider the online tools that you use to present the databases. In order to make prudent decisions you will need to obtain more accurate and representative use data and calculate Return on Investment profiles. This more precise evidence of the most valuable databases will allow you to retain the best tools and demonstrate that other databases are not high priorities for future renewal.

You have already read the literature and worked with other collection development librarians at annual conferences to develop methods that identify coverage overlaps. You have also uncovered associated methods to measure value based upon use and cost-per-use data. What you need to concentrate on for the next ten months is creating better web-based pathways to resources so your future use data reflects the best resources you provide.

After meeting with the subject librarians, it is determined that you will work closely with the web support staff, the electronic services librarian, and the web development team to enhance the web site pointers to the databases. In addition to revising the way researchers access the databases from the general pages, the subject pages, and the campus portal, you will attempt to provide a solution that will offer the advanced functionality and flexibility in web page design that the subject liaisons have requested, plus the automatic capture of web use data for evaluation, reporting and planning, and for making additional web site revisions. The domain of the initial investigation has grown significantly, and you now have additional team members. The data you require for your decision process will be produced and the expanded effort will also provide a broad range of associated enhancements. All members of the investigation team are excited by the possibilities and are more than willing to expend the effort required to find mutually beneficial solutions to long-standing difficulties.

Perhaps you spoke too rashly. After meeting with the web support team it seems they expressed reservations about the scope of the investigation and the realistic possibilities of modifying the web site so dramatically. The web team did not seem to fully understand and appreciate the frustrations of the liaison librarians.

Another meeting was held between the public services liaison librarians and the web support team to discuss the situation in greater detail. The initial conversation was quite tense as each side was attacking and defensive at the same time. The web support team initially displayed sensitivity to any criticisms of the system. The group calmly reviewed the passionate reactions, and with the assistance of the neutral head of collection development as a facilitator, they were able to explore and identify underlying issues that were causing some of the reservations. The group eventually uncovered interests that revolved around pride and control issues with the existing system. It was also obvious that the web support group had little understanding of the patron needs that were unmet by this rather strict web presentation software. In their minds the system was able to display the required alphabetical and subject lists of databases. They had even managed to create ways to highlight special databases at the top of the lists. They learned of librarian and user frustrations due to the limited display options. After some discussion and demonstration of exemplar web pages from other libraries, they were able to understand the desires for page sections, free form annotations, RSS channels, and embedded widgets for providing chat options and scrolling news. Another important recognition was the desire to move toward customized pages with subject-specific elements presented based upon user characteristics that were passed on to the library as part of the validation process. Even the ability to emphasize various page elements using CSS (Cascading Style Sheets) controls and user characteristics was envisioned as future enhancements. In terms of control, the web support group was satisfied that the initial review of more flexible web pages and sites had enough structure and still contained the basic elements they required for authority and site-wide navigation.

During this meeting the liaison librarians gained a much better appreciation for the support efforts that occurred in the background to keep even the basic tools functioning, and the long list of requested enhancements that the web support team was asked to develop while absorbing reductions in staff, equipment, and software. By the end of the meeting there was a much greater understanding of the issues and intentions, and a willingness to work together to find new approaches. It was now time to start scanning for best practices.

The full project description and plan was released to the entire library for review and comments. A number of people responded that they had no idea that the situation was so complex and that they felt far more aware of the entire issue as a result. They offered to provide any type of support that was required. Two other staff members mentioned that they were aware of similar investigations that were either already completed or still underway in other libraries, and provided contacts for the team.

A fairly comprehensive environmental scan, consisting of literature reviews, web site reviews, personal communications, and site visits produced the following clusters of example web page design and support practices for further consideration.

The first cluster of options was based upon manually created HTML5 pages using templates for style and structure. The pages were very flexible if the designer was familiar with advanced coding and functionality options. Because of this functionality and flexibility, the overall web site design required significant attention as the infrastructure would change radically if new types of tools were introduced. A team of designated staff were always exploring and introducing new web features and training the page authors. Complex non-linear relationships could be developed between databases, providing multiple paths to the best databases for a particular question, but each link was managed as a unique feature and duplicate links had to be updated by a person on the web support team at the server level in order to simultaneously update all similar links on the site. The static nature of the pages meant there would be significant amounts of redundant updates to changing elements unless a database was created to dynamically maintain and update the underlying links. There were some Drupal databases in operation, but the integration of HTML5 and Drupal was not yet sufficient for easy implementation by a small web support staff. The analytics software used on this site provided basic transaction logs, but did not offer much in the way of built-in analysis of the captured use data. This approach offered the desired flexibility but not enough infrastructure to provide low maintenance technical support or the required levels of monitoring, capture and analysis of sophisticated use data.

The group reviewed this scenario and agreed that the bare minimum solution should contain some sort of locally maintained background database for economies of scale, ease of updates, and use data capture and analysis. It was agreed that the recent reductions in resources would result in very limited staff time and few new servers or software that allow for the development of such new options. That meant the review of potential platform and software solutions was limited to two basic approaches.

The first alternative was represented by the ColdFusion software package. This was a database-driven solution that generated pages dynamically, in real time based upon calls to the server. There were numerous examples of powerful and impressive web sites based upon this approach. The support for current and future functionality was handled by the commercial company with assistance from user group participants. The joint efforts produced sites that utilized a variety of templates to established standard elements but also allowed for flexibility. The customization options were most developed in areas where all participants agreed on priorities. The service options were impressive, the underlying database provided efficient maintenance, and the data capture was adequate for basic analysis. This approach provided the essential needs, with the only disturbing limitation being the inability to customize the presentation of materials without either strong local systems support or perhaps total user group agreement.

The second alternative support model was exemplified by the LibGuides software, part of a growing suite of software that offers a nice balance of the previously desired features plus interesting add-ons that support testing, reference chat with associated transaction log capture, and the ability to use reference chat answers and other manually input data to create an online FAQ (Frequently Asked Questions) tool. These added value options were seen as even more important because integrated service elements were now desirable. The existing suite of support tools required regular tweaking for compatibility, and it was recently learned that some tools such as the Meebo chat software will soon disappear after many customizations were made. The team was excited to have seamlessly integrated tools that were reliable and which offered advanced analysis and service options.

One additional service option that was discovered as the result of this environmental scan was the concept of Pathway tracking as an important evaluation tool. This approach is utilized by a number of organizations to add layers of advanced analysis to simple page hit counts. Some software tools allow you to monitor sequential links by an individual, in this way showing pathways along a logical sequence which arrives at a desired information or tool page, as opposed to sequences which appear to stop at deadend pages that are probably showing frustrating failures to locate the intended tools or information. Studying these pathways allows an organization to look for problematic or missing directional links and to modify existing links within the non-linear web environment. This pathway analysis immediately uncovered some unexpected but popular entrances to a web site and discovered problem deadends that could be corrected or adjusted. This is a powerful type of user feedback without the need to intrude upon the user experience and would serve as a helpful supplement to regular focus group and user observation sessions. This is just one example of the many unintended enhancements that can be discovered during a supposedly targeted review project.

Not only did this scan for best practices provide a series of possible options which will lead to a better implementation and an even more responsive library, but it also demonstrated to stakeholders and key decision makers that the library encourages daring explorations that produce transformational successes. These successes are recorded for internal staff as Lessons Learned documentation to provide examples for future brainstorming, and each success encourages more aggressive questions leading to further transformational change. As a collection, these shared decision-making exercises show action across traditional silos, provide rewards and recognition for great ideas and actions, and re-emphasize the support for a system of continual review, searching for best practices, and carefully monitoring any modifications for indications of impact.

Another result of obvious success is that there will be greater expectations for phenomenal enhancements the next time. Also be prepared for site visits, as you will become the exemplar institution for this service. Quite often such recognition and networking lead to additional enhancements as other seekers share their discoveries.

6

Key management skills that contribute to organizational leadership and direction

Abstract: Management is an underappreciated activity – especially when it is done well. A superb manager appears to be "running a well-oiled machine". However, that machine does not operate in a smooth and effective manner by accident or by momentum. An organization tends to protect its existing structure and operation, so adjustments and refinements require attention, consideration, planning, and coordination. Leaders must have vision, budget skills, personnel skills, creativity, compassion, approachability, and persuasive if not charismatic techniques. A good leader is consistent and determined, and has the ability to take responsibility, delegate responsibility, prioritize when resources are inadequate, and has the courage to drop services when they are no longer of high value to the larger organization.

Key words: management, managers, skills, planning, budgets, personnel, communication, delegation, persuasion, courage, leadership.

Normal staff attention to tasks

In general, hard-working people concentrate on performing assigned tasks as effectively as possible, hoping for as few interruptions and surprises as possible. Excellent performance is measured and demonstrated through productivity and efficiency and little time is spent contemplating how to improve or redesign operations and services in response to outside influences. Only exceptional circumstances will cause most staff members to explore the larger implications of intruding external pressures.

Administration attention to efficiencies and effectiveness

In most organizations the administration is charged with reviewing the overall appropriateness and effectiveness of an organization or its parts. In many organizations the administration is seen as out-of-touch with daily operations and poor at communicating positive feedback. Administrators are often seen as bean counters and critical reviewers with unreasonable expectations rather than facilitators, advocates, and mentors. Many administrators were excellent performers who were promoted to administrative positions with few training opportunities to develop administrative skills. It is no wonder that many new supervisors and administrators experience initial failures which erode the confidence of both themselves and their staff. It is also not surprising that untrained administrators do not develop powerful toolkits for handling the many types of circumstances they will face. New managers are often learning on the job, utilizing spontaneous crisis management techniques and relying on the assistance of a few exceptional performers to cover the problems that appear in the unit.

Shared responsibility for reviews and improvements

What is required for good management is a perspective of continuous service quality improvement, with full participation of all affected staff. This is how an organization balances long-term satisfaction and effectiveness targets with the short-term productivity concerns. The best decisions are made when the most informed personnel are involved in reviewing current operations. Enhanced services result from considering future modifications to existing operations and services, whether they are identified as obvious candidates for immediate attention or reviewed during regular scans of operations.

Comparing internal policies, procedures, productivity, and user satisfaction results to outside benchmarks is a good way to ensure you are not complacent with functioning operations, but that you are striving for the best practices and highest levels of service. Performing environmental scans takes time and effort, as does an internal review, but the long-term benefit far exceeds the loss of productivity due to disruption. An involved and empowered staff creates a more flexible and agile organization, a high performing organization where morale is raised, communication is improved, and everyone feels they understand how they play a part in accomplishing the Mission of the organization. These skills and conditions are significant qualitative benefits that are necessary for organizational health, and total staff involvement and organizational understanding are measurable goals to be met even if your reviews themselves do not always generate savings and/or enhancements to services.

Leadership skills

Managers require a large and diverse set of skills in order to perform effectively. Only through a combination of training and experience will these talents be merged into a polished presentation. Great leaders are not born complete; some people naturally inspire confidence, but instinct can only carry you so far when you face complex problems. A shallow or inadequate manager will quickly be exposed as unaware, unprepared, or overwhelmed, but a great leader will both facilitate and provide vision and creativity. Developing a suite of tools and techniques will allow a natural leader to continue to impress co-workers and to facilitate a team toward higher levels of performance.

Under the best of circumstances it is difficult to introduce change into an organization, even when it is clearly needed, and only a trusted leader with a well-developed team of managers and an energized staff can make this transformation happen relatively smoothly and successfully. Some of the traits that are important if one is to function as a leader as well as a coordinator or facilitator are described below.

Vision, based upon experience

The first thing a leader must have is a Vision. One cannot lead effectively if there is no initial path or destination to travel toward. This Vision and associated plans are developed from a combination of three key elements: experience, knowledge, and skills. Experience by itself does not guarantee awareness and expertise. While looking is natural, seeing is an intentional act that requires attention and contemplation. The act of paying attention and attempting to fit new observations into your existing world view is what generates understanding and knowledge; many people can tell you what they saw, but few can integrate these experiences into a revised intellectual model. Leaders have the mental ability to incorporate new experiences and concepts and to utilize these additional elements in solving new problems. But it requires more than observation and memory to be a leader, you must also develop a sharp intellect and a set of powerful skills and tools to recognize and analyze each situation appropriately. Vision is seeing a thing clearly, understanding the implications, and acting correctly and proactively in a timely manner. It is being one step ahead of others because of a blend of preparation, intellect, and exploration.

Conflict aversion means high priority

Some managers are conflict averse, and their initial behavior is to avoid making difficult decisions. It is important to remember that inaction is an action. Not making a decision assigns an existing service to the Do category, which means it remains a high priority. This avoidance action may result in the inappropriate use of limited resources when it results in continuing Do-level support for an already questioned service. At the least, assigning a questioned service to the Delegate category means that someone will be responsible for evaluating the operation and its value.

Quick adaptability

Of course any destination is approximate and likely to be altered over time. Think of good leaders like experienced sailors, pointing toward a destination, but aware that circumstances may require a change of course and force adaptations to the original goal. A wise leader is always searching for, and very early becomes aware of, conditions that might alter plans in mid-adventure.

Creativity

Being aware, prepared, and inquisitive is not enough to ensure good leadership, one must also be creative. Powers of creativity are not born, but rather developed, and Creative people exhibit traits that allow them to cultivate novel ideas and solutions. An open mind is essential for gathering data and ideas, as exploration of what might at first appear to be outrageous possibilities is the most likely way to achieve transformational rather than transitional or incremental change. Maintaining a sense of fun in the workplace is also a way to allow random ideas to percolate and be introduced into a strict organizational mindset. Thinking from the point of view of the user also allows a person to escape the operational mode and enter into the desirable services mode. This user-orientation is especially important as external influences impact user expectations more quickly than they register on internal processes. Looking for outside trends helps a leader discover new possibilities that might be applicable for their industry. For example, imagine how incorporating crowd-sourcing and folksonomy behaviors that are prevalent in other internet services might allow for exciting new social networking access points to materials and also create new community advocates for library services.

Workplace opportunities for creativity and exploration

In addition to personal orientations, there are important workplace conditions that should be encouraged in order to generate creative ideas in an organization. Creativity comes from experience and confidence, so an organization should emphasize the delegation of authority to enterprising staff members as a means of teaching and mentoring leadership and project management skills. Allowing staff to generate and propose solutions and alternative approaches, with appropriate oversight and coaching, will develop a stronger organizational ability to identify opportunities for creative problem solving. Thinking about new approaches encourages new approaches, so emphasize and support an organizational culture of continuing education. Develop programs that promote new ideas and highlight new trends, tools and techniques; keep staff interested in new ideas and reward exploration. Provide a listening environment, a safe place where all ideas are allowed to be described and explored fully before any restrictions are placed on conversations and respect alternative approaches and perspectives. Continually ask for suggestions and provide a risk-free environment for all staff to toss out radical ideas as part of a learning atmosphere. Many organizations say that they respect alternative thinking, but it is important to actually promote meeting behaviors that provide an atmosphere of exploration and creativity.

In reality, few organizations see much blue-sky thinking expressed by staff if speaking encouraging words is all managers do to promote such "strange" behavior. In order to make staff comfortable in such circumstances it is necessary for leaders to exhibit such exploratory behaviors themselves. Many managers start meetings by presenting a previously developed solution and then ask for comments. In such situations, the stake is already planted in the ground and any constructive alternatives are often seen as criticisms. Instead, managers should provide a description of the key conditions and ask for ideas leading to solutions. This will allow informed staff members to provide perspectives and alternatives in a setting that encourages creativity. This more free-form approach may take a bit more time to develop solutions, but the solutions themselves may be more interesting, the ideas and information raised during the planning may prove beneficial for other purposes, and staff will learn a great deal more about the operational priorities, the organizational resources, and the best ways to present ideas for future conversations. The administration's long-term goals are actually better served by providing a think tank environment rather than by providing an immediate solution. A considered solution developed in the open by a group is often more persuasive than a presented solution, even if the ultimate efficiency and economy are equal. When an organization is under time and/or fiscal pressures the dedication to group creativity is even more obvious and more recognized.

Inspiration

You can be aware, prepared, and open to creativity – but another element is important to moving an organization toward becoming as a high-performing team. That driving force is inspiration. If momentum keeps an organization conservative, and structure and culture position an organization to seek new approaches, the jump start for such creativity comes from individual sparks of interest and excitement. Such propulsion comes from inspired individuals who feel comfortable asking questions in a safe environment. The best way to create an inspirational organization is to be an inspiring leader.

Staff willingly follow a person when they trust and admire their intellect, their skills, and their behaviors. A good leader is one who demonstrates an understanding of the full range of requirements and capabilities within an organization and who is able to understand and speak to the elements of the work done by each employee – if not be able to perform every task – which is not always reasonable in a very large organization. Respect is given when one has demonstrated respect for another.

Having an honest conversation, with complete attention given to another person, is the best way to generate trust and develop a personal relationship that will pay dividends in both directions over time. It is impossible to overestimate the importance of personal interactions and the impressions they make based upon a sense of shared dignity, humility, and sensitivity to personal concerns. While politicians and greedy leaders will say anything at any time to win approval, an inspirational leader will always be seen as consistent; rather than pivot their beliefs and support based upon local interests, they will demonstrate a sense of fairness in all circumstances. While they will on occasion advocate for groups and individuals after balanced considerations, they will always approach decisions from an overall organizational frame of reference. A leader will speak for the group, listen to the group, and give credit for teamwork where deserved. Leaders succeed when people follow them willingly, rather than by pushing people in a particular direction. You can feel when an organization has an inspirational leader, or a team of inspirational leaders because such unmistakable positive energy leads to teamwork, excitement, innovation, and improvements, even in difficult circumstances.

Sensitivity

A manager may have tremendous abilities in many of the areas listed above – vision, inspiration, creativity, analytics, communication, and persuasion – but will not be as successful as possible without one additional trait: approachability. A great leader is personable and humane, exhibiting understanding, a positive attitude, a sense of the importance of mentoring, and the ability to be brutally honest when appropriate. The best managers are exemplars of dignity and productivity tempered by humanity and understanding. A superb manager is someone you can talk to about any topic without fear of judgmental reactions and with assurances of maintaining complete confidences when requested. When times are tough and pressure is felt, you need to be able to trust your managers to understand the circumstances and have the organization's best interest as the paramount concern.

Finding a person with highly developed skills and attributes in all the areas listed above is rare, and you should feel very lucky if you work for a superb manager and leader. While managers should strive to constantly improve in all areas, there are a few traits that deserve the most immediate attention and a few skills that deserve concentrated development. These are the skills that will be the most essential when dealing with difficult fiscal scenarios requiring tough decisions.

Be firm and clear in designations

Clear designations of activity categories for every task are important for both staff and external stakeholders. Firm and unmistakable decisions will provide messages about commitment, vision, priorities, leadership, and teamwork. Nebulous conditions will create mixed signals, uncertainty, fear, and unnecessary internal competitions and conflicts. This uncertainty may also create unpredictable and distracting mid-course resource re-allocations that will need constant attention and interventions. Waffling and indecisive priorities may also divide the support of your external advocates, making your organization appear to be a less obvious central and holistic service.

Courage in convictions under difficult circumstances

Many administrators have good observational skills, can analyze situations well, and are capable of making wise allocation decisions based on current priorities and resources. The tools and skills are at their disposal to effectively lead an organization through normal and difficult times. What may be missing that would make someone a great leader is a clear vision and plan that remains in place regardless of the changing and challenging circumstances. A vision becomes a reality when a leader exists who can remain focused and creative in order to keep on track. Many managers quickly modify their well-developed goals by allowing environmental conditions to dictate their actions, which shows a lack of perseverance and consistency in their decision-making.

Reassurance and addressing team feedback

Only when there is continuous reassurance and support from the administration, the project managers, and library-wide managers will an organization embrace change and support new and uncomfortable efforts in a meaningful way. For this reason it is important to regularly survey an organization for signs of understanding, provide encouraging progress reports, and solicit feedback. A good leader regularly communicates new ideas, encourages participation and creative solutions, and listens and reacts to organizational feedback. A team effort is difficult to coordinate and complete and therefore requires more intentional and consistent leadership and monitoring.

Remaining cognizant of the ultimate goals, diligent in supporting the priority needs of the project, and remembering the dire implications of losing focus in terms of reaching your aspirational vision, makes it easier to stay with the original program as distractions threaten the success of your initiative.

Assessment skills

Preparation, understanding, and teamwork are necessary ingredients for successful management, but these are merely the conditions desired for facilitating enlightened management. Good management requires a set of assessment skills that channel the internal resources that have been developed and positioned through careful climate creation. Two of the most essential management skills to develop are fiscal management and staff assessment.

Fiscal management

Fiscal management is necessary in order to evaluate existing operations, to reconsider priorities, and to perhaps re-allocate limited resources to maximum advantage. A brilliant vision and empowered staff are most effective when given appropriate resources to complete a well-designed task. Effective managers can chart operations, match workflows to resources, develop evaluation methods, and show Return on Investment (ROI) figures for each portion of their operation. With this knowledge in hand, it is then possible to compare these known costs and services to stakeholder desires and priorities. You may have an effective operation, but the cost compared to the value may not be a wise investment, given other possible services of higher value to your user population. As conditions change it is necessary to re-evaluate the costs compared to new options such as outsourcing for efficiencies, reducing costs by accepting different end-product standards, and accepting alternative services. It is also appropriate to consider removing long-performed services if the costs are too high compared to other desired services. This purposeful abandonment decision may be difficult to accept for emotional reasons, but it is easier to justify and defend if you have solid fiscal evidence about actual costs and benefits.

Fiscal management does not stop at measuring the costs of existing operations and services. Effective and proactive managers study patterns and generate cost projections that influence future directions. What appears to be a slight deterioration of service quality compared to increasing costs this year may become a major drain on operations over the course of the next five years. Creative uses of small annual roll-over balances may allow for the development of contingency funds or planned project funds over a period of years, while developing plans for accumulating technology replacement funds on a regular basis will avoid large drains in years when new software and hardware upgrades are required.

Operational costs and expenditures are often mysterious to those staff not directly involved in budget preparation, so providing maximum transparency with budget information creates a more informed and trusting organization. This deeper understanding of the financial circumstances and competing requests for support will foster greater empathy and acceptance if/when personal or unit requests are not approved. Managers should provide relevant fiscal information when responding to suggestions – whether they are approved, postponed, or denied; there is great value in understanding what priorities are considered higher when you do not receive additional resources. This additional information may make it easier to write a more powerful justification if a request for support will be submitted again in the future. Denied staff may not agree with the ultimate decision, but they will be more accepting of the situation if they understand the fiscal and priority decisions that lead to allocation decisions. When looking at morale factors, understanding and acceptance of present fiscal limitations that delay additional support is always a better response to an unsuccessful request for resources than resignation or frustration, which is frequently the result of unpopular decisions arrived at through unknown decision processes.

Personnel management

Skillfully managing a budget means effectively distributing fiscal resources, but good management also requires the ability to maximize personnel: having adequate resources and the correct people concentrating on the highest priorities is the key to success. As operations change or new services are introduced, new skills are required, and previous skills may be de-emphasized or phased out. Existing staff must be prepared to adapt to these new expectations, and new staff must be hired to provide entirely new sets of skills. Under such circumstances regular reviews of staff capabilities are in order. Managers must perform non-threatening staff assessments, provide appropriate training to address gaps when discovered or created, offer significant motivation and rewards for staff development, and make staff re-allocations and re-assignments when necessary to maximize existing personnel skills and capabilities and to minimize the negative impacts that may arise from inappropriate assignments.

Personnel management is as much art as science, with sensitivity and personality as important as facts, figures and logic. Managers are most effective when appealing to people's innate sense of wonder and pride in their efforts. Spending the time necessary to understand a person's interests and potentials is a key to creating a strong and flexible organization. Quite often a person with limited experience may have the required orientation to contribute significantly to a project or exploration. Perceptive managers may find people who are in positions that under-utilize their skills, and this may allow for expanded opportunities, organizational benefits, and the development of new managers and leaders among the experienced staff. In actuality, most people do not start in positions that maximize their skills, so providing growth opportunities makes sense for both the organization and the individual. People who experience success and advancement within an organization will bring out the best in others, assuming they are adequately trained and encouraged in this direction. There is no more powerful change agent than a successful employee who has advanced due to creativity and opportunity.

Successful managers lead change by effectively promoting, encouraging, and receiving support for enhancing an organization's influence and services. Persuasive leaders present their organizations as dynamic, responsive, and effective. Winning the trust and support of inside and outside stakeholders is often the direct result of demonstrating previous success and innovation. It helps if the presenter is charismatic, but a strong presentation can be made by natural introverts if the content is impressive and the vision is inspiring. Presentations, be they in formal settings or in an impromptu elevator ride, should be both succinct and meaningful to your audience. When communicating with busy stakeholders remember that less is more – grab their attention using emotions and utilize imagination to obtain commitments. Data is useful for supporting positions and answering detailed questions, but a powerful argument is won with impressions and ideas.

The four Ds: Do, Delegate, Delay, Drop

When leading an organization or a project, it is important to understand the limits of resources. Failure may result from a brilliant plan if it does not receive adequate support. A good manager knows how to allocate limited resources based upon realistic expectations. Short-term stresses on a system may result in higher productivity or higher level services, but ultimately stress will degrade the organization through exposing underlying weaknesses or creating staff burn-out.

In order to protect the quality of services, and the health of the staff, a good manager reviews every possible operation and places each under one of four categories of activity. The categories are, in order of priority: Do, Delegate, Delay, and Drop.

■ **Do** means the task leader takes responsibility for the accomplishment of the goals with existing resources. There are measurable objectives that should be met on a specific timetable, and any problems should be highlighted and addressed immediately. The goals can be across the continuum from theoretically developing a plan of action all the way to implementing a quality service, but the effort is given the highest possible priority.

- **Delegate** means the task is assigned to another person for completion. The task has value and priority, but the responsibility for oversight is given to another person or group. It is not the priority task of the top-level manager, but the top manager should provide adequate resources, expect regular progress reports, and be available to discuss concerns if success appears problematic. Mentoring is expected as opportunities for creativity and new skills and tools become necessary and/or available. Success is both reaching the goal and learning about higher levels of management and organizational coordination.

- **Delay** means the task has been determined to be of lesser importance than those currently receiving support. It does not imply lesser value, but simply less immediate value toward the selected strategic initiatives. Delay classification may mean a task is shelved for the present moment, and is placed in the parking lot for future reconsideration. It may also mean that the organization chooses to postpone an existing operation for a designated period of time or until certain conditions appear. It is important for a manager to keep these Delay decisions on the agenda so as not to lose sight of them as conditions change and priorities are re-examined. These are good ideas that deserve reconsideration. It might even be beneficial to assign each idea to a champion who reports back on the topic during the next review period.

- **Drop** means the value of the service is no longer important enough to warrant consideration. The task may have value, but it is not important enough to the stakeholders to deserve continuing attention and resources. This is where Purposeful Abandonment is implemented. Despite organizational momentum, emotional attachments, historical experience, and even particular champions, the service value is deemed unsupportable given present resources and other expectations. Expect some push-back from internal and external players, and even some surprising populations with irrational and difficult-to-counter positions. Be prepared to demonstrate the factors involved in the decision in a reasoned way. Recognize the sensitivities involved, but emphasize the larger perspective of gaining the greatest amount of good from the resources involved. In general, do not promise to reconsider the Drop decision in the future. If reconsideration was realistically desired in the future you would be placing the service in the Delay category. Be clear to internal and external stakeholders in your intention to no longer support this service. A difficult decision should only be made and supported once; do not repeatedly drain your limited fiscal and emotional resources revisiting well-considered decisions.

Top priorities remain unchanged

Once a strategic plan has been developed, it is essential that the leadership maintain commitment to the designated goals. Regardless of financial or staffing changes, stakeholder priorities will remain the same – which means satisfaction will still be measured by successfully reaching the initially determined measurable objectives. Fewer resources should not mean modifying the targets unless there are very serious changes in circumstances that completely alter user preferences. There may be required delays in order to reach initial targets, but the end-product should remain unchanged. At most, the relative priorities among the initial targets might be reconsidered, as the highest priorities receive more resources to keep them on the initial timeline.

Lower service priorities remain in basic support mode

If the strategic plan was performed realistically there should only be a few top priorities and these should still be important enough for concentrated effort and special resource allocations. The important, but lesser, priorities should already have been isolated and supported at adequate levels for acceptable performance. These basic service levels should not need to be modified unless you are now required to abandon or severely alter all existing services. Basic operations should continue for the period of the strategic plan without much added attention. Remaining focused on the top priority enhancements is the key to moving forward.

Focus and faith to stay the course

Success in reaching the goals of the organization requires total group involvement and focus. Regardless of surprises and distractions, good leaders keep teams focused. They convince all participants of the importance of the immediate goals and assure staff that other competing concerns can be delayed and no negative effects will occur due to temporary disruptions to regular operations. This message of understanding and long-term vision must be transmitted throughout the organization in order to garner the type of cross-unit collaboration and cooperation that will support special circumstances.

Prior feedback from stakeholders before suspending a service

Choosing to suspend or end a service is sometimes the right decision, but any significant policy or procedure modifications should not be enacted without first soliciting stakeholder feedback. Placing an existing service in the Delay category without performing a service review may anger those expecting services. A potentially very dangerous way of determining importance is not to involve stakeholders in the Delay decision, and then rely on not hearing any complaints after suspending operations. Likewise, Dropping services without consulting potential stakeholders may prove disastrous, even if the service itself carries little actual value. The perception of ending a particular service is often more significant than the importance of the service itself. Be sure to recognize and consider the symbolic impact of these decisions.

Build in reviews after a fair trial period

While some decisions will never need to be reconsidered, many may require or incorporate later review. During the project management phase, and through the review period, it is important to commit to a fair test. Unless there are gross miscalculations, it is best to stick to your plans until scheduled reviews demonstrate that there are required modifications. Do not tinker with designed operations unless significant efficiencies or satisfaction issues arise. It takes time for operations to reach smooth levels of effectiveness, and there will be initial frustrations from internal and external participants, perhaps even unreasonable venting from some affected parties. Trust in your long-term plans and let time demonstrate the quality of your decision-making team efforts.

After a reasonable amount of time has passed, be sure to review the progress of your efforts. Look for indications of success, be they enhanced services, recovered resources, better coordination and communication, proactive management, or leadership development. Use these decision and project reviews to fine tune your decision-making processes, your suite of tools and techniques, and your organizational commitment to shared service quality review efforts. Not every decision will be perfect, nor will every project reach completion as originally designed, but each effort will be a step toward creating a stronger learning organization.

Harness internal power

Management is a team effort, although there must be an authority for making ultimate decisions in situations where no clear consensus is possible. This team thinking is best accomplished when an organization creates tools that allow for the most effective sharing of information and knowledge. The more easily people can gather data and previously learned experiences and lessons, the quicker and better will be the quality of the conversations and the decisions. Well prepared agendas that provide essential supporting materials and clearly specify intended actions and outcomes will facilitate timely and thorough group deliberations and decisions.

Knowledge Management practices can assist an organization in these capture, mining, and sharing efforts; software and practices can be used to handle and re-purpose information for competitive advantage; and enterprise-wide tools such as SharePoint and Drupal-based intranets can help by enhancing organizational communication and collaboration. These tools allow large populations to store, organize, retrieve, and re-purpose captured knowledge, thereby saving time and effort, reducing redundancy, providing benchmarks and assessment histories, storing oral histories, and maximizing local expertise. By its very nature and mission, a library is perfectly positioned to utilize these tools and demonstrate to outside decision-makers the value and ROI of supporting such information-handling efforts.

Demonstrate the change you want to promote

Libraries should serve as micro-demonstrations of the power of participatory management and information-sharing principles. By effectively handling difficult situations as a team, and including outside stakeholders in the process, the library can convince key decision-makers of the importance and the potential influence of the library and its resources in assisting in coordinating and maximizing the greater organization's future decision-making processes and directions.

Stand on the shoulders of teammates

A unified and effective organization demands attention and respect. A manager is only as successful as his/her team, and a good leader is seen through the reflection of his/her staff opinions. The real and perceived power of a manager is in the apparent successes of their operation, which is dependent on a well trained, well respected, and well supported team of smoothly integrated individuals.

In the following case, a request for inclusion by one element of the staff generates an honest review of all existing authority and responsibility roles. Issues such as supervision, communication, teamwork, union compliance, problem solving, fairness, historical culture, trust, and planning were raised. Deliberations resulted in revised policies and procedures that improved all aspects of the situation, enhanced the organization's ability to be flexible and agile, and clarified the roles and responsibilities of all staff in maintaining a continual service improvement culture.

Case Study 11: Shared governance

Shared governance, the involvement of all staff in organizational decision-making, creates great opportunities and also great potential challenges when compared to traditional top-down hierarchical management. Depending upon how well an organization has prepared its staff to be meaningful participants, you may witness a wide range of results from exceptionally creative and delightful cooperation through total confusion and paralysis. As in any complex situation, to achieve maximum benefits it is essential that all involved operate with shared interests, similar understandings of the resources at their disposal, an awareness of any external conditions that might present barriers or conflicts, a shared vocabulary that describes clear expectations for decision-making processes and responsibilities, support for addressing concerns in a transparent way, and trust that all opinions and ideas will receive a fair and respectful hearing.

In this case, a new civil service council has announced that they wish to become involved in the management of the library, specifically in reviewing and developing best practices and resolving long-standing grievances. They state that they have little confidence in the ability of either the existing administrative hierarchy or the powerful faculty librarian council to adequately represent their concerns, or to even effectively manage the library due to long-standing irregularities and conflicts which have created many library-wide problem situations that need to be reviewed and revised. They believe that integrating their concerns into conversations may actually help the library break the deadlock that now seems to prohibit much creative and responsive management.

To set the scene, here is a summary of the existing dysfunctional leadership situation. Currently there is a tenuous balance of authority between the administration and the faculty council which is charged "to advise on all directions" and is responsible for tenure, promotion, and periodic faculty retention decisions. There exists a void where there should be a consistent and shared vision due to constant conflicts based upon protecting special internal interests rather than focusing on user-oriented services. In terms of daily operations based upon a strategic plan, there is great difficulty in setting short and medium-term directions and priorities for services and facilities modifications due to years of conflict-averse behavior by the former administrators. This failure of the administration to assume legitimate authority and leadership responsibilities, combined with additional failures to address accountability concerns, resulted in a situation in which the concerned faculty librarians began to exert significant influence into areas which had previously only operated with administrative oversight. The administrative neglect also resulted in a failure to maintain policies and procedures documentation, and over time further confusions regarding leadership roles within increasingly complex scenarios. Operations continued, but there was little serious attention to regular reviews and improvements as long as no crises arose.

A new and more accountable administration had recently arrived and was attempting to reassert its authority over daily operations, implement service quality evaluations and enhancements, and to increase its influence in determining the future direction of the library. Needless to say, years of experience under the previous conditions had led to misunderstandings and improper habits from both parties that would need to be discussed in open and honest meetings. That type of calm, thoughtful, directed conversation had never been maintained for long enough to make significant progress due to the many pressing situations that appeared and demanded more immediate attention. The staff across the library seemed to have resigned themselves to a situation that contained enormous tension, uncertainty, mistrust, and endless surprises due to poor communication and planning.

Despite these unhealthy conditions, the library managed to offer many state-of-the-art services. What was missing was staff engagement in assessment and program planning. As a result of very little emphasis on measuring the satisfaction of present services or systematically exploring future service enhancements, there had been small modifications to existing services and crisis management corrections to address problematic situations, but there were no regular service reviews or environmental scans leading to proactive testing and early adoption of new tools and techniques before they became industry standards. In addition, very little customization of generic services had been implemented because there was little underlying investigation and assessment that identified the values of locally tailored possibilities.

In terms of turning to the user population for feedback, there was not even a Student Advisory Committee in place to accept feedback. Only the University Senate Faculty Library Committee provided feedback, and they rarely met and had no real impact. The power to drive decisions more often rested upon the ability of the faculty librarians to influence their constituents in the University Senate, which made resource allocation decision recommendations to the campus administration. However, these relationships did not exert much influence on daily operations or strategic planning. To the majority of library users, with no special expectations, the library appeared to be running smoothly. To the intensive library users with concerns about having access to the most current and effective library services it appeared that there were internal issues that were creating unnecessary barriers, and that even the library staff were frustrated and seemed resigned to this situation. Key campus administrators were aware of the internal chaos, as it had ultimately become such a morale and public problem that it required the removal of the previous administration.

Turning to present day behaviors, limited experience with the benefits of programmatic analysis, accountability, and delegated authority has made many faculty librarians suspicious of what they see as bean counter administrators who would be better utilized by simply facilitating the existing priorities and services. Due to this isolation from best practices at other libraries, there is little awareness of, or contemplation of, some new industry trends that should be explored. While many new services were introduced during this time of librarian faculty influence, a noted lack of regular reporting or formal recording of the historical progress and modifications makes recognition difficult.

The success of the library is in large part the direct result of relying on exceptional teamwork and altruistic extra effort by the librarians and some of the dedicated civil service staff, but the continuing losses of staff and reductions in resources are making the situation untenable. It is simply not possible to continue to perform all the traditional services plus adopt the many new approaches being suggested with the diminished level of resources. While the faculty librarians have repeatedly claimed they need additional resources, they have not provided the requested justifications and documentation to make persuasive requests.

The faculty librarians were asked to create arguments for new resources based upon measurable impacts expected as direct consequences of reduced service levels. Unfortunately, this measurable impact would be quite difficult to demonstrate initially as no previous measurements of service quality or satisfaction were gathered. Faculty librarian frustrations grow more obvious with every new reduction in resources, but no new approaches or strong documentation has been produced. Instead the faculty librarians blame the continuing deterioration of conditions on the inadequacy of the administration to provide support.

The administration has repeatedly asked for documentation of effort, results, and evidence of impacts plus testimonials. They insist that they cannot develop powerful justifications for new resources based upon feelings of being overworked, especially when they repeatedly reference earlier staffing levels without recognizing the significant changes in the industry that have provided very different types of self-help and a reduced need for intermediary staff. Attempts at tracking efforts and effectiveness are seen as hostile and wasted efforts. Attempts to demonstrate the power and necessity of strong evidence-based proposals when requesting additional resources from higher administrators have failed to produce new behaviors or supporting materials. As expected, the lack of evidence and quantifiable outcomes in previous requests has been met with no successes in obtaining additional resources.

The spiral of frustration and entrenchment only makes this situation worse. Both sides are striving for similar user-oriented results, but they cannot seem to work together to take the necessary steps to reach their shared goals. Their special interests, often hidden, make collaboration very difficult. In some cases good ideas are abandoned or not supported so as not to give credit to the other side in the event of success.

The administration had recently realized that their good intentions were often seen as attempts to add additional tasks to already stressed individuals and units, and they decided to phrase any new requests for supporting information about efforts as attempts to identify services that could be reduced or purposefully abandoned if their priority was not high from the user point of view. The hope was to demonstrate understanding and empathy while trying to resolve some real misunderstandings.

Now that you have a better understanding of the conditions, let us look at the issue of setting future directions. One key unresolved issue that frequently rises to the surface during especially stressful times, such as those caused by staff reductions or designations of priority services, is the role of the administration in setting directions for the library. In this case, the faculty librarians have stated that the role of the administration is simply to facilitate current processes. The faculty librarians claim that it is the role of the faculty to set directions in the library just as faculty do in all other teaching colleges. They maintain this belief despite the specific statement in their faculty by-laws that they are to "advise the administration" and participate in the hiring and review of faculty. This difference of opinion about appropriate responsibilities for creating the libraries future directions becomes particularly obvious in situations that involve large resource allocation consequences such as technology adoption. Attempts to find a compromise position frequently fail and discussions about necessary and timely solutions degrade into passionate defenses of perspectives and definitions about the true nature of shared governance. Entrenched positions on authority rights now frequently stop any meaningful attempts to find resolutions to real problems, and also deepen the existing quagmire.

These continuing and conflicting interest-based perspectives have created tension and great distrust among the entire staff, with the civil service members never quite sure where to turn for advice or for support. The reconstitution of the defunct civil service council was a direct consequence of this uncertainty. The previous civil service council was disbanded when the union was approved, with the belief that the union representatives would be able to negotiate and communicate on behalf of the civil service staff. Unfortunately, while the union representatives were able to adequately address certain contract issues such as fair evaluations and consistent application of policies and procedures, they were not positioned or trained to be effective representatives for contributing to conversations about daily operational concerns and setting future directions. The council was seen as a way to more directly influence operations and to be proactive and involved in early discussions rather than reactive to later-stage proposals of potential modifications to library priorities. Of course the council would also add another layer of special interests into the already confused and contentious deliberations.

Perhaps the necessity to document the current decision-making practices for the new civil service council members might provide an opportunity to seriously review the existing situation, and to expose all established and new special interests that will be operating under the surface. Given the history and the complexities involved, it would probably be advantageous to involve a consultant, or at least a neutral facilitator, in this process. Let us now look at some of the steps required to address and correct the existing difficulties.

The first action required is to create documentation about the existing policies and procedures, including a list of parties responsible for the accountability and enhancement of each area. In some areas there may be a designated individual due to their assigned position responsibilities, while in other areas review and enhancement may be the responsibility of a standing committee or an ad hoc task force. This assignment of responsibilities is different than identifying parties interested in assisting managers in order to develop the best possible services. Responsibility for a particular task or service is also different than being part of a group that determines the priorities across all library services.

Once individual service responsibilities are clear it is time to document and publicize service goals, priorities, and measurable objectives, and to expect that regularly scheduled service reviews are made to the appropriate operations and policy review committees. All related unit goals and individual objectives across the library to support each effort should be recorded and reviewed on a regular basis by both the individual unit supervisors and higher-level service coordinators. This step will clarify the alignment of each service with the Mission, the relationship of supporting units, and the responsibilities for planning and maintaining each associated task. At this point the individual service managers should publicize ways in which other interested parties throughout the library can contribute toward continual service reviews of their areas.

Now that the management of individual tasks is clear, it is time to concentrate on the delicate balancing of resources across these services. In many ways this is the real driver of future directions for the library, and these broad conversations should be isolated from the special interests of the individual units. Parties discussing library-wide goals and resource allocations should be expected to restrain their emphasis on their own unit priorities in favor of library-wide user-oriented priorities. This is the level at which all staff have the greatest opportunity to be involved in influencing the future directions of the library. Informed opinions from across all library units and staff levels should have input into decisions that will have significant impacts and affect the entire library. The difficulty is not in finding volunteers to express their opinions, but rather in developing informed and fair participants.

Shared governance requires the right people, with the right information and the right attitude, to listen and collaborate in order to find the best balance of interests that satisfies the stated Mission of the organization. The interests of the users should always remain the most important interests at the table. This is best accomplished by having the strategic objectives phrased in terms of user services, and aligned with stakeholder preferences and realistic resources. Keeping them visible at all times on the wall during meetings is a great way to reinforce this approach.

It is important to make a place at the library leadership table for all staff groups to contribute in order to both capture the greatest amount of perspective and creativity – and to establish the broadest sense of shared accountability. After experiencing the advantages of such broad representation, this expanded membership approach will quickly cascade down to the other cross-library groups that are charged to investigate, review, and propose enhancements to individual library operations as a continuing responsibility. But just having a seat at the table does not ensure equal opportunity for influence. There are rules that must be established to make these meetings productive.

A set of formal behavior expectations is helpful for new members of a group, and can serve to train and maintain proper behavior in situations where special interests run high. Particular emphasis should be placed on treating every person and every idea as worthy of consideration without interruption. Another important understanding is when agenda items are intended for gathering information as opposed to deciding upon issues. A final important behavior expectation is that each person should become aware of how to appropriately handle difficult situations using a clearly understood set of procedural rules that will avoid accusations of unfair manipulation of situations. If each member feels they are being treated fairly and equally they are more likely to be honest and creative.

To quickly move past potential hidden blockages, start each new agenda item by recognizing all existing and underlying interests (both within the library and from outside) that might interfere with effective shared decision-making. You cannot completely remove these interests, but you can work as a group to recognize them, and work together to emphasize the user-oriented interests as the higher priority as you continue exploring solutions. It helps to use Interest Based Problem Solving techniques to uncover deeply hidden concerns, as well as to be certain you are addressing the actual cause rather than superficial symptoms. Maintaining a shared focus is a key to productivity.

Even with the best of intentions, information, and awareness, diverse groups will not always be able to find mutually satisfying compromise solutions. The group must agree at the outset to be satisfied with many shared victories, but to be prepared to occasionally win or lose on specific issues, knowing that in the long run there will be a fair balance on settling directly conflicting issues using user-oriented solutions as the preferred targets. This long-term understanding of the priority of user interests as the final arbiter is absolutely necessary in order to maintain trust.

Finally, to maintain a safe and dignified environment, all members must agree to publicly support the results of votes as the best possible compromise under the circumstances, and not to engage in hidden subversive actions that will undermine the good faith efforts of their peers. Discussing the issues that were considered is allowable, but sharing private information or disclosing member positions is not appropriate professional behavior. Make the new civil service staff members comfortable and proud to be a part of a positive and respected team.

As with any other operation, the efforts and decisions of the leadership group should be documented and made available for public discussion. Celebrate the successes, discuss the complications in hopes of finding better compromises or novel solutions, and treat the history of the group as lessons to be learned in order to build the type of trust and shared responsibilities that are the hallmark of high-performing organizations.

Conclusion

The most important D: Do

Having now considered the previous pages, which are full of reminders and suggestions for being a creative and graceful leader during difficult financial times, it is time for you to embrace the tools and techniques that will work best in your particular organization in order to be an enlightened manager and an effective leader.

Working with others, develop or refine your Vision, document your strategic priorities, publicize your immediate goals and measurable objectives, seek out and adopt best practices, and establish a culture of continual service quality reviews. Be an effective advocate for your organization to outside stakeholders, and be an example of decorum within your organization.

It is never too soon or too late to share your knowledge and skills and involve others in designing and refining a higher performing organization. Your well-considered guidance will be even more appreciated during times of financial strain and reduced resources, when emotions are most likely to cloud reasoned considerations and alter the normal balance of internal special interests and user-oriented services.

Do not wait complacently for crises to appear, or avoid making tough decisions that will eventually demonstrate your failure to provide timely and proactive services. Take action, be accessible, and constantly refine and improve services and morale. Be a problem solver and an effective and respected leader.

Appendix A

Start-up scenarios to ponder

As you assimilate the content you have just read, it might be useful to perform some active learning techniques to gain some less stressful experience with these approaches before you attempt to implement them under pressure in a public setting. As an exercise to demonstrate your ability to identify powerful methods that are appropriate for specific situations, attempt to map out the best techniques from the text in order to address the issues that might arise in the following scenarios. The act of making your own outlines will reinforce your understanding, generate skills that will become natural, and increase your confidence in your ability to think on your feet through recalling and utilizing prior experiences.

1. New Director

As the new chief administrator you will want to gather opinions, review policies and procedures, identify best practices, and become familiar with recent internal annual reviews and unit service reviews, retreat reports, and consultant reports. You will want to scan the Mission statement and see how well it aligns with the annual goal priorities (strategic plans), budget histories, and documented reallocation patterns (with the associated justifications for new or revised funds). You will also want to review any collected user and outside stakeholder opinions, existing LibQUAL+ reports, and any other user survey results. You will want to review or begin to implement environmental scans for new possibilities, and relate these options to public service standards and expectations. Finally, you will want to support continual service quality reviews, and involve users and stakeholders as feedback sources and potential advocates.

2. New Unit Head

As the party responsible for maintaining efficient, effective, and creative operations toward a particular user-oriented service, you will want to perform all the review tasks that a new Director would undertake in order to understand your operations within the larger library context. You will also connect with other unit heads to understand the inter-relationships, collaborations, and potential impacts of modifications to your operations on other units. In addition, you will want to concentrate on reviewing personnel files for unusual conditions and identifying high potential employees who can assist you in understanding the local conditions. You will want to lead environmental scans for new possibilities, review and revise your service expectations and measurable objectives, and review the present service quality compared to industry benchmarks. Finally, you will want to meet with your key users and stakeholders to involve them in service reviews and to develop them as strong advocates for future endeavors.

3. New responsibilities for outside liaison efforts

As a person assigned to develop and maintain relationships with outside partners and user populations, you will want to understand who your current and potential users and collaborators are, determine how involved they are, and how aware they already are, of current and potential library services. Contact unit heads and subject liaisons to identify existing relationships, and scan the industry to uncover novel and non-traditional populations who are being served in other organizations. Gather opinions and impressions from outside stakeholders about the present library services and performance, and then demonstrate additional possibilities and determine what new services they desire that might be implemented. Work with library staff to explore the costs and feasibility of these new services. Then using these estimates, evaluate these new service costs along with existing service costs in order to calculate the potential return on investment for each process. This analysis may lead to joint library–stakeholder reconsideration of priorities, and perhaps Purposeful Abandonment of some services in order to support newer and more valued services. Maintain regular contact with your outside partners and user populations in order to obtain feedback about their satisfaction with working arrangements, the coordination of related and shared services, and library performance compared to stated expectations. Consider these populations as not only service recipients or partners, but also as ambassadors and advocates for obtaining additional resources to develop enhanced library services. The users are our ultimate raison d'etre, and they should feel involved and influential in shaping our goals and measuring our success.

Appendix B

Suggested readings

The following book will provide an excellent introduction to the subject of library assessment, preparing you to design and implement continuous service reviews.

Matthews, Joseph R. *The Evaluation and Measurement of Library Services*. Westport, CT: Libraries Unlimited, 2007. Print.
An excellent introduction to evaluation and measurement of library services, containing summaries of prior research and bibliographies, overviews of techniques, and areas for exploration.

Philosophical

The following books and articles provide various philosophical overviews to the concepts of organizational cultures, qualitative and quantitative library assessment, analysis methods, and practical implementation strategies.

Collins, Tim. "The Current Budget Environment and Its Impact on Libraries, Publishers and Vendors." *From Surviving to Thriving: Building Blocks of Success*. Special issue of *Journal of Library Administration* 52.1 (2012): 18–35. Special Issue: Print. Also doi 10.1080/01930826.2012.630643.

Based upon a broad survey, the article addresses reactions, primarily movement to electronic materials and PDA approach, and mentions hesitancy to programatically reduce staffing, but instead to use opportunistic attrition.

Harbo, K., and T. Hansen, Getting to Know Library Users' Needs — Experimental Ways to User-centered Library Innovation. *LIBER Quarterly* 21.3/4 (2012): 367–385. And *http://liber.library.uu.nl/index.php/lq/article/view/8031/8392*

Describes how to become more aware of, and how to consider library services from a user-oriented perspective.

Harper, Shaun R., and George D. Kuh. "Myths and Misconceptions about Using Qualitative Methods in Assessment." *New Directions for Institutional Research*, 136 (2007): 5–14.

Outlines the concerns and importance of qualitative data when appropriately used.

Hernon, Peter and Ellen Altman. *Assessing Service Quality: Satisfying the Expectations of Library Customers.* Chicago: American Library Association, 1998. Print.

This introduction to service quality presents a balance of philosophical concerns, techniques, and examples to assist managers in distinguishing between user satisfaction and user-oriented service quality assessment.

Hernon, Peter, Robert E. Dugan, and Danuta A. Nitecki. *Engaging in Evaluation and Assessment Research.* Santa Barbara, CA: Libraries Unlimited, 2011. Print.

Discusses how to conduct library research by highlighting the research process, the role of research design, the collection and analysis of data, and presentation of findings that inform management decision-making.

Hiller, Steve and Stephanie Wright. "Turning results into action: using assessment information to improve library performance." *Proceedings of the 2008 Library Assessment Conference: Building Effective, Sustainable, Practical Assessment* (2009), pp. 245–252. Print. And *http://libraryassessment.org/bm~doc/proceedings-lac-2008.pdf*

Part of the bi-annual Library Assessment Conference: Building Effective, Sustainable, Practical Assessment, with the goal "to build and further a vibrant library assessment community by bringing together interested practitioners and researchers who have responsibility or interest in the broad field of library assessment." *http://libraryassessment. org/index.shtml*

Horowitz, Lisa R. "Assessing Library Services: A Practical Guide for the Nonexpert." *Library Leadership and Management* 23.4 (2009): 193–203. Print.

Excellent overview of the important considerations, with a brief bibliography and Appendix: Performance Guidelines and Standards for Comparison.

Lakos, Amos, and Shelley E. Phipps. "Creating a Culture of Assessment: A Catalyst for Organizational Change." *Libraries and the Academy* 4.3 (2004): 345–361. Print.

An early call for preparing an organization to accept and adopt assessment as a cultural perspective.

Shaughnessy, Thomas W., ed. "Perspectives on Quality in Libraries." *Library Trends* 44.3 (Winter 1996): 459–678. Print.

Ten contributions are included that consider a variety of perspectives and scenarios.

Matthews, Joseph R. *Library Assessment in Higher Education*. Westport, CT: Libraries Unlimited, 2007. Print.

A review of the assessment process in academic library settings, providing a philosophical underpinning, but not specific tools and techniques.

Nicholson, Scott. "A Conceptual Framework for the Holistic Measurement and Cumulative Evaluation of Library Services." *Journal of Documentation* 60.2 (2004): 164–182. Print.

A philosophical review of various user perspectives and key measurement topics.

Ninopal, Jennifer. "Project Portfolio Management for Academic Libraries: A Gentle Introduction." *College & Research Libraries* 73.4 (2012): 379–389. Print.

Describes PPM as a way to ensure that a suite of limited duration projects align with organizational missions and priorities, and have appropriate attention and resources for successful completion. Discusses the cultural and practical considerations when introducing such a tracking process into libraries.

Saracevic, Tefko, and Paul B. Kantor. "Studying the Value of Library and Information Services. Part I. Establishing a Theoretical Framework." *Journal of the American Society for Information Science* 48.6 (1997): 527–542. Print.

First of a two-part publication which addresses the philosophical aspects, definitions, and proposes models of quality and value for library and information services.

Saracevic, Tefko, and Paul B. Kantor. "Studying the Value of Library and Information Services. Part II. Methodology and Taxonomy." *Journal of the American Society for Information Science* 48.6 (1997): 543–563. Print.

Part two discusses a framework for a taxonomy of values and user assessment methods.

Snelson, Pamela. "Communicating the Value of Academic Libraries." *C&RL News* 67.8 (2006): 490–492. Print.
ACRL President's call for greater understanding of how to evaluate library value that is meaningful to chief academic officers.

Urquhart, Christine. "How Do I Measure the Impact of My Service?" *Evidence-Based Practice for Information Professionals*. Ed. Andrew Booth and A. Brice, 210–222. London: Facet, 2004. Print.
Discusses the complexities of determining quantitative impact assessments.

Urquhart, D. J. "Economic Analysis of Information Services." *Journal of Documentation* 32.2 (1976): 123–125. Print.
An opinion piece on whether it is possible to create an economics of information transfer.

VanDuinkerken, Wyoma, and Pixey Anne Mosley. *The Challenge of Library Management: Leading with Emotional Engagement*. Chicago: American Library Association. 2011. Print.
Discusses many challenges facing forward-thinking organizations when addressing cultural and personal factors that arise from working in a continuous change environment. Contains thoughtful considerations of techniques for staff engagement, planning, and addressing unexpected disruptions. Includes example scenarios.

White, Herbert S. "Cost-Effectiveness and Cost-Benefit Determinations in Special Libraries." *Special Libraries* 70.4 (1979): 163–169. Print.
Early call for studies showing the perception and appearance of corporate library value despite the

overhead scenario which makes a meaningful cost–benefit analysis difficult.

Whitehall, Tom. "Value in Library and Information Management: A Review." *Library Management* 16.4 (1995): 3–11. Print.

Provides an economic analysis framework for library services, and methods of measuring value, usefulness, and effectiveness benefits.

Worrell, Diane. "The Learning Organization: Management Theory for the Information Age or New Age Fad?" *Journal of Academic Librarianship* (1995): 351–357.

Discusses the concept of libraries as learning organizations, highlighting the organizational culture elements, utilizing library-wide staff knowledge and open dialog, using data for problem solving, and employing systems thinking for the planning processes.

Measurement

The following books and articles provide various analysis methods, explanations, example tools, and approaches to performing qualitative and quantitative library assessment and value determination.

Botha, E., R. Erasmus, and M. Van Deventer. "Evaluating the Impact of a Special Library and Information Service." *Journal of Librarianship and Information Science* 41.2 (2009): 108–123. Print.

Demonstrates an impact analysis of library services based upon focus groups, interviews, and short surveys from a group of natural sciences researchers.

Brophy, Peter. *Measuring Library Performance: Principles and Techniques*. London: Facet, 2006.

A clear overview of issues in performance measurement from a strong user-oriented perspective.

Cornell University Library. *Cornell University Library Research and Assessment Unit: Making Data Make Sense.* *http://research.library.cornell.edu/data*
The Research and Assessment Unit assembles and reports relevant data, both qualitative and quantitative, to achieve two main goals: first to help address a wide range of questions about how best to align library programs with user needs, and second to report on library performance. Pointers exist to local information and to selected national library statistical data sets.

Dougherty, Richard M. "Assessment + Analysis = Accountability." *College & Research Libraries*, (2009): 417–418. Print.
A call for the use of quantitative methods to demonstrate library value and effectiveness.

Gerlich, Bella Karr, and G. Lynn Berard. "Testing the Viability of the READ Scale (Reference Effort Assessment Data): Qualitative Statistics for Academic Reference Services." *College & Research Libraries* 71.2 (2010): 116–137. Print.
Provides an interesting way to measure the quality and requirements of reference questions.

Hiller, Steve and James Self. "From Measurement to Management: Using Data Wisely for Planning and Decision-making." *Library Trends* 53.1 (2004): 129–155. Print.
An overview of historical library data collection and analysis methods. Contains an excellent bibliography of early activities.

Hernon, Peter and Ellen Altman, *Assessing Service Quality: Satisfying the Expectations of Library Customers.* Chicago: ALA, 1998. Print.

In this work they "describe how to assess service quality with a focus on library users and explain how to define performance standards, and when to use certain kinds of tools."

Joubert, Douglas J., and Tamera P Lee. "Empowering Your Institution Through Assessment." *Journal of the Medical Library Association* 95.1 (2007): 46–53. Print.

The study has some LibQUAL+ assessment information, but it is best for highlighting the importance of a culture of assessment.

Kaufman, Paula and Sarah Barbara Watstein, "Library Value (Return On Investment, ROI) and the Challenge of Placing a Value on Public Services." *Reference Services Review* 36.3 (2008): 226–231. Print.

A significant attempt to quantify the value of library services.

Kyrillidou, Martha and Colleen Cook. "The Evolution of Measurement and Evaluation of Libraries: A Perspective from the Association of Research Libraries." *Library Trends* 56.4 (2008): 888–909. Print.

Provides an historical perspective on ARL measurement and evaluation approaches and programs, with a strong emphasis on the work of W. Lancaster.

Lewin, Heather S. and Sarah M. Passonneau. "An Analysis of Academic Research Libraries Assessment Data: A Look at Professional Models and Benchmarking Data." *Journal of Academic Librarianship* 38.2 (March 2012): 85–93. Print.

A study of ARL activities related to public availability of assessment data, with three exemplary sites highlighted.

Li, Xin, and Zsuzsa Koltay. *Impact Measures in Research Libraries: SPEC KIT 318*. Washington, D.C.: Association of Research Libraries, 2010. Print.

An attempt to determine best practices, with very little actual product discovered.

Markless, Sharon, and David Streatfield. *Evaluating the Impact of Your Library*. London: Facet, 2006. Print.

An excellent overview and beginner's guide for developing and implementing impact studies.

Matthews, Joseph R. "What's the Return on ROI? The Benefits and Challenges of Calculating Your Library's Return on Investment." *Library Leadership & Management* 25.1 (2011): 1–14. Print.

Shows how to calculate value for public library services based upon direct and indirect benefits.

Oakleaf, Megan. "Are They Learning? Are We? Learning Outcomes and the Academic Library." *Library Quarterly* 81.1 (2011): 61–82. Print.

This article considers six questions relevant to the assessment challenges librarians face in coming years: (1) How committed are librarians to student learning? (2) What do librarians want students to learn? (3) How do librarians document student learning? (4) How committed are librarians to their own learning? (5) What do librarians need to learn? (6) How can librarians document their own learning? Helps librarians consider how to utilize assessment plans in order to articulate their value and better position themselves for integration into the larger organization.

Oakleaf, Megan. *Value of Academic Libraries: A Comprehensive Research Review and Report. Association of College and Research Libraries*. Chicago: Association of College and Research Libraries, 2010. *www.acrl.ala. org/value* or *http://www.ala.org/acrl/sites/ala.org.acrl/ files/content/issues/value/val_report.pdf*

Helps libraries define instruction outcomes, demonstrating institutional value by measuring the degree to which they attain institutional outcomes. Discusses how to establish, assess, and link academic library outcomes to institutional outcomes related to the following areas: student enrollment, student retention and graduation rates, student success, student achievement, student learning, student engagement, faculty research productivity, faculty teaching, service, and overarching institutional quality. The bibliography section has a long list of previous studies.

Poll, Roswitha. "Impact/Outcome Measures for Libraries." *Liber Quarterly* 13 (2003): 329–342. Print.

An early article describing the need for evidence-based analysis, and

Li, Xin, and Zsuzsa Koltay. *Impact Measures in Research Libraries: SPEC KIT 318.* Washington, D.C.: Association of Research Libraries, 2010. Print.

Follow-up attempt to determine actual impact evaluations and to promote best practices templates – unfortunately, the authors found too few examples to provide significant assistance.

Poll, Roswitha. "Quality Measures for Special Libraries." *World Library and Information Congress: 73rd IFLA General Conference and Council.* Oslo, 2007. Print.

Discussion of performance indicators in special libraries.

Poll, Roswitha, and Philip Payne. "Impact Measures for Library and Information Services." *Library Hi Tec* 24.4 (2006): 547–562. Print.

Discusses and demonstrates the impact/outcome method in library evaluation.

Rubin, Rhea Joyce. *Demonstrating Results: Using Outcome Measurement in Your Library*. Chicago: American Library Association, 2006. Print.

A practical guide, containing example forms, for developing outcome measurement techniques as they contribute to the planning process. Focused on public libraries, but valuable for all managers.

Scharf, Meg. "Tellin' Our Story—Or Not: Assessment Results on Academic Library Web Sites." ACRL 14th National Conference, Seattle, WA. March 13, 2009. *http://www.ala.org/acrl/sites/ala.org.acrl/files/content/conferences/confsandpreconfs/national/seattle/papers/192.pdf*

A study of the presence of assessment and use data on library web sites.

Schonfeld, Roger C., and Ross Housewright. *Faculty Survey 2009: Key Strategic Insights for Libraries, Publishers, and Societies*. Ithaka, 2010. Published April 17, 2010. *http://www.sr.ithaka.org/research-publications/faculty-survey-2009*

This fourth in a series of surveys conducted over the past decade examines faculty attitudes and behaviors on key library issues. Supplemented by a survey of library directors. *http://www.sr.ithaka.org/research-publications/library-survey-2010*

Self, Jim. "Using Data to Make Choices: The Balanced Scorecard at the University of Virginia Library." *ARL: A Bimonthly Newsletter of Research Library Issues and Actions* 230/231 (2003): 2. Print.

See also current scorecard metrics at *www.lib.virginia.edu/bsc/* (accessed March 22, 2009).

Thompson, Bruce, Colleen Cook, and Martha Kyrillidou. "Concurrent Validity of LibQUAL+ Scores: What do LibQUAL+ Scores Measure?" *Journal of Academic Librarianship* 31.6 (2005): 517–522. Print.

Describes how this standard evaluation tool measures satisfaction more strongly than outcomes.

Tools

The following tools provide examples of assessment methods.

Balanced Scorecard
http://www.balancedscorecard.org/BSCResources/Aboutthe BalancedScorecard/tabid/55/Default.aspx
"The Balanced Scorecard is a strategic planning and management system used to align business activities to the vision and strategy of the organization, improve internal and external communications, and monitor organizational performance against strategic goals. It was originated by Drs. Robert Kaplan (Harvard Business School) and David Norton as a performance measurement framework that added strategic non-financial performance measures to traditional financial metrics to give managers and executives a more 'balanced' view of organizational performance. The 'new' balanced scorecard transforms an organization's strategic plan from an attractive but passive document into the 'marching orders' for the organization on a daily basis. It provides a framework that not only provides performance measurements, but helps planners identify what should be done and measured. It enables executives to truly execute their strategies."

The use of this tool is discussed in collaboration with the Malcolm Baldrige Criteria to assess service quality in: Wilson, Despina Dapias and Theresa del Tufo and Anne

E.C. Norman, *The Measure of Library Excellence: Linking the Malcolm Baldrige Criteria and Balanced Scorecard Methods to Assess Service Quality*. Jefferson, N.C.: McFarland, 2008.

http://www.countingopinions.com/
"Counting Opinions provides software that enables an organization to: continuously obtain customer opinions, automatically analyze and rank customer-identified opportunities for improvement, and continuously monitor the impact of an organization's ongoing actions aimed at improving its customers' satisfaction."

They offer LibSat for customer satisfaction measures and LibPASS for performance data analysis.

The Lib-Value Project
http://libvalue.cci.utk.edu/content/lib-value-project
"Faced with difficult economic times and university budget cuts, the value of the library to the wider goals of the university is increasingly questioned. Return on investment (ROI) measures are a concrete means of demonstrating to institution administrators and public audiences the vital role academic libraries hold within both their respective communities and on a global scale. While libraries have traditionally been rather modest about broadcasting their own worth, today they must learn to make clear the often unrecognized ways in which they contribute to institutional success. This demonstration of value is exactly what Lib-Value, an IMLS-funded grant project, aims to empower."

LibQUAL+
http://www.libqual.org/home
"LibQUAL+® is a suite of services that libraries use to solicit, track, understand, and act upon users' opinions of service quality. These services are offered to the library

community by the Association of Research Libraries (ARL). The program's centerpiece is a rigorously tested Web-based survey bundled with training that helps libraries assess and improve library services, change organizational culture, and market the library. The goals of LibQUAL+® are to: Foster a culture of excellence in providing library service, Help libraries better understand user perceptions of library service quality, Collect and interpret library user feedback systematically over time, Provide libraries with comparable assessment information from peer institutions, Identify best practices in library service, and Enhance library staff members' analytical skills for interpreting and acting on data."

Project SAILS (Standardized Assessment of Information Literacy Skills), a service of Kent State University
https://www.projectsails.org/Home
"Project SAILS is a knowledge test with multiple-choice questions targeting a variety of information literacy skills. These test items are based on the ACRL Information Literacy Competency Standards for Higher Education. The SAILS test offers universities and colleges a method for testing the information literacy skills of its students. Beginning June 1, 2012, the cost is $4.00 per student up to a cap of $4,000 per administration. For up to 5,000 students. If you are testing more than 5,000 students, please contact SAILS for pricing."

Index